Pictorial History of
the University of Virginia

PICTORIAL HISTORY
of the University of Virginia

William B. O'Neal

The University Press of Virginia
Charlottesville

Foreword

In order to control the hundreds of prints and photographs that clamored for a place in this pictorial history of the University of Virginia, it soon became obvious that a strict plan was needed and that strict adherence to that plan was absolutely necessary. Time, on the other hand, fell quite naturally into four divisions —the conception of the University (1819–1825); its beginning splendor (1825–1861); its survival and consolidation (1865–1917); and its expansion (1918–the present). But the real problem was what to include and, even more important, what to exclude, in each section of the people and places that were important to that section.

Since the University is unique in two ways – it was designed by its founder and most of its founder's drawings for it have survived—it seemed best to devote a certain amount of space to Thomas Jefferson and his designs. At the same time the original Board of Visitors was so remarkable and the first distinguished guests of the University so eminent that it seemed they, too, should be included. This decision, in turn, set a pattern that could be followed throughout the book. That is, only guests of great eminence, such as Lafayette or U.S. Presidents, should be included, and only the first faculty, just as only the first Board of Visitors, need be pictured, although donors are included wherever possible.

Unfortunately, three of the presidential guests do not seem to have been photographed while they were at the University. Grover Cleveland spoke before a statewide assemblage here in 1885; William H. Taft gave a series of lectures; and Theodore Roosevelt had a hunting lodge not far away (see Illus. 1),

1. Pine Knot, lodge of President Theodore Roosevelt near Charlottesville 191504

and on at least one of his visits to the area, he spoke to the alumni and faculty. He also expressed "a keen interest in the practical success" of a fund-raising effort launched by the University at the time of the centennial of the Louisiana Purchase, a project started under the sponsorship of Robert Lee Preston and Thomas Nelson Page.

As for buildings, those designed by Jefferson have been shown many times under many circumstances. They deserve this multiple inclusion, for they, too, are unique in the history of educational building and are one of the few undoubted architectural masterpieces our country has produced. Beyond that, many of the vanished buildings have been included in an attempt to furnish the reader with the material necessary to re-create the University at any of its more important moments. Of the contemporary buildings that make up so much of today's University, it is impossible to show more than a small fraction. Importance of design or importance of the function housed has been the guide here.

Students are both the cause and the purpose of any university. Since it seemed wise to indulge in the doctrine of firsts in the case of the Board of Visitors and the faculty, so it is that Poe is the first and only student to be picked out individually, although Woodrow Wilson, an alumnus, is shown as a student, but because of his presidential rank rather than his alumni status. And other students are included in reunion or class groups or as athletes.

This policy, of course, excludes many famous alumni and is a particularly frustrating aspect of the space limitations of this book. One of the most notable examples of this sort of omission is that of Walter Reed, who graduated from the University with his M.D. at the age of 17 in 1869 (see Illus. 2). He then went on to earn a second M.D. at Bellevue Hospital, New York, and in 1874 joined the army medical corps. By 1893 he was professor of bacteriology and clinical microscopy at the Army medical school, while in 1899 he and his assistant were detailed to study yellow fever. Reed's theory that the mosquito was the sole carrier of the disease was triumphantly proved, but, neglecting his own health, he died in 1902 from chronic appendicitis.

Student activities, on the other hand, have been used as much as possible, and student organizations, with their symbols when

2. Walter Reed

available, have been listed in chronological order in the sections that cover the dates of their foundation. Those that have been included are the Greek letter, the honorary, and the professional groups.

The reader's indulgence must be asked for omissions. Space limitations prevent the inclusion of many pictures of great interest that may even fall within the strict canons necessarily adopted. But the exclusion of many hundreds of other photographs saddens the author perhaps even more than it may the reader. One photograph, at least, was excluded from the text for reasons of modesty, that of the University Press of Virginia, which has helped so greatly with instituting and producing this book. Established in 1963, the Press has rapidly become one of the strong agencies at the University for the dissemination of its, and Virginia's, learning. In 1967 the Press was able to move into permanent quarters in Bemiss House, named in honor of Samuel Merrifield Bemiss, a member of the first board of the Press as well as one of its strongest animators, whose family gave substantial assistance in the remodeling of these new quarters.

Numerous people have helped in the writing of this book. President Edgar F. Shannon, Jr., gave valuable information about Carr's Hill; Victor Reynolds, Director of the University Press of Virginia, has generously aided it in every possible way; indeed, the entire staff at the Press has smoothed the difficulties of its production enormously; and William Weaver, my research assistant, Mrs. Edwin M. Betts, whose collection of prints and photographs of the University is so extensive, Miss Anna Barringer, Miss Anne Freudenberg, Edmund Berkeley, Jr., and Gus Hamblett have all been most energetic in helping to solve the problems of research that arose. I am most grateful to all of them and to Francis L. Berkeley, Jr., who has put his broad knowledge of the University at my disposal.

I recognize that there may be exceptions even to the simple rules laid down for this fond look at the University of Virginia, but exceptions sometimes enliven a concept. Finally, any mistakes that may be found, and when one deals with so many facts mistakes inevitably occur, are entirely my responsibility. For these I apologize in advance.

Any continuing institution does not stop at a specific date in time, and so it is with the University. Even in the period between the writing and the publication of such a book as this, changes, sometimes great ones, occur. It is, then, only possible to stop, not finish, this manuscript, for the story of the University is an endless one that will continue as the University continues to expand and delight future generations of students.

W.B.O.

Charlottesville, 1968

Contents

Pictorial History of
the University of Virginia

Introduction

Before the Legislature granted a charter for the University of Virginia, Thomas Jefferson and his fellow board members had begun building a collegiate community in Charlottesville. This earlier institution was known first as Albemarle Academy and subsequently was chartered by the Assembly as Central College. These establishments had been formed in order to take advantage of the monies that the Commonwealth was beginning to distribute from the Literary Fund, a fund which is still in existence, though it is currently used only for the public school system. Private subscriptions had enabled the board of Central College to buy land and to begin building a college to match Jefferson's ambitious plans, ambitious both educationally and architecturally. The present Pavilion VII, West Lawn, was the first of the buildings to be started; its cornerstone was laid on October 6, 1817.

In 1818 the Assembly appropriated $15,000 to found a state university and appointed a commission, with Jefferson as chairman, to select a site, choose plans, and work out its operation. The commission met August 1, at Rockfish Gap in the Blue Ridge Mountains (see Illus. 3). Thomas Perkins Abernethy points out, in his *Historical Sketch of the University of Virginia*, that "the selection of Rockfish Gap as the place of meeting was

3. Rockfish Tavern on Afton Mountain

significant, but the selection of Jefferson as chairman was decisive. He used all his arts to push the claim of his native Albemarle, stressing especially its central location and its salubrious climate. Central College offered all its assets as an inducement," and in 1819 the General Assembly chartered the University of Virginia, to be established at the site of Central College, which was to merge with the new University.

It is necessary to point out that neither Albemarle Academy nor Central College ever had a student, held a class, or possessed a faculty member. They both existed only as administrative units, and, although Central College possessed a number of buildings that had been started, it is doubtful that any of them had been finished by the time the Assembly granted its charter in 1819. It should also be pointed out that the Assembly, at the same time it granted the University its charter, also adopted Jefferson's plan for Central College as the official plan for the University. The adoption of the Rockfish Gap Commission's report, then, was a complete triumph for Jefferson—his county was chosen as the site for the new University, his designs, some already in the process of execution, were approved for the new institution, and he was chosen as a member of the new Board of Visitors, which, in turn, promptly chose him as Rector, a position from which he could supervise not only the building operations at the University but also the choice and quality of the faculty, the contents of the new library, and the courses of study for the students.

Sixty-eight students arrived for the opening of classes on March 7, 1825, a total of 123 entered between then and the end of the first session, and the average number for the first seventeen years was 191. Although Jefferson lived until July 4, 1826, and thus saw the first classes in operation, his death in actuality ended the era of the formation of the ideas on which the University, architecturally and educationally, was founded.

To the Board of Visitors, the faculty, and the students, then, fell the task of beginning the University in such a way that it would be a permanent success. At first none of these three groups seemed to be able either to govern or to coexist with one another, but as solutions to problems were found the pattern peculiar to the University emerged, a pattern which has carried through, in part, until the present.

By the 1850's both the need and the possibility for new buildings appeared and a wave of expansion began. The principal building of this group was, of course, the Annex to the Rotunda. Monroe Hill was enlarged, while Dawson's Row and the Infirmary completed this wave of enlargement. Modest as these additions may seem to us, they made the University, before the Civil War, one of the largest in the country and the cost per session to the student more than that of Harvard, Yale, or Princeton.

The coming of the Civil War ended this second phase of the University's development. Its announcement is most dramatically described by an alumnus writing in 1889:

Immediately after the Presidential election of November, 1860, many of the students assembled and formed a company of Volunteers, which was organized early in that month. The Company was made up of the very best material this great Virginia school contained at that time, consisting of 120 members. . . .

The company after organization drilled every day, on the University Lawn, and by reason of the intelligence of its members was soon almost perfect in the manual of arms, as well as in the evolutions of company and battalion drill. . . .

These boys drilled every evening, from the middle of November, '60, till the middle of April, '61.

After this company which was called "The Southern Guards," was organized, a second company was formed. . . .

During the exciting times in the winter and spring of '61, nothing was talked of in the social gatherings in the halls of the Literary Societies, or in the meetings of the military organizations, but the political situation, and the fast approaching clash of arms.

According to custom, Jefferson's birthday was celebrated at the School founded by that great man, and it was arranged that a battalion drill should take place on the evening of that day, in which drill and parade all the military companies of Charlottesville and the University should participate. . . .

There were four companies. . . .

In all there were some four hundred men handsomely uniformed and well equipped. By request of the commissioned officers of the four companies, the writer of this was asked to take command of the battalion on that occasion.

The battalion drill begun about four o'clock on the 13th of April, 1861, and was witnessed by an immense concourse of people assembled on the Lawn.

The drill being ended, the battalion was drawn up in line for dress

ered a facet of expansion. After the war a great rush of students returned, no less than 5,119 in the 1947–48 session, a figure which now seems low in view of the more than 8,600 who attended the University in 1967–68.

The last vestiges of rurality have disappeared in the University's measures to care for these increasing numbers, while Charlottesville, which had begun as a village a mile or more away, now has flowed around the grounds. Thus, although the Lawn with its buildings by Jefferson remains the center of the University both physically and spiritually, subcenters are springing up. The new University Hall is one with its huge mass dominating the landscape around it and, happily, providing a new focus for what had been the nondescript area of emergency housing for married students, the housing, like all temporary measures, having lasted no less than twenty years. Another such center will soon appear on the Duke land when the new buildings for the School of Law and the Graduate School of Business Administration are built. And a third will inevitably arise on the Birdwood acres recently acquired for future use.

If the physical history of the University has been one of controlled growth, that growth has not prevented it from using the talents of outstanding architects—including Benjamin Henry Latrobe, Dr. William Thornton, Robert Mills, Stanford White, Fiske Kimball, and Pietro Belluschi—in the process of transforming itself from Jefferson's small but triumphant grouping into its present widespread facilities. But surely Jefferson's spirit has animated this expansion throughout, for it has always been given impetus in order to care for the educational needs of the University's students and never from the desire for mere size.

The University Is Conceived
1819–1825

191504

4. Thomas Jefferson, *ca.* 1799–1800,
probably by Benjamin Henry
Latrobe

Thomas Jefferson
1743–1826
Father of the University of
Virginia

This portrait drawing in pencil of
Jefferson is almost certainly by
Benjamin Henry Latrobe, although absolute documentary
proof is lacking. It was probably
drawn in Philadelphia during the
winter of 1799–1800.

5. Engraving by B. Tanner of the University of Virginia, 1827

Engraving of the University of Virginia in 1827

This 1827 view shows the new University with its original roof scheme intact. The parapets on Pavilions III, V, IX, VIII, and X, the flat roofs on the dormitories, and the original railings give the Lawn a much greater neoclassic look than it has had since the disappearance of these features.

The engraving is taken from a map of Virginia, "constructed in conformity to Law, from the late Surveys authorized by the Legislature and other original and authentic Documents by Herman Böÿe." The map was engraved by H. S. Tanner, but the engraving of the University was executed by B. Tanner.

6. The Edgehill portrait of Jefferson, 1805, by Gilbert Stuart

The Edgehill Portrait of Jefferson

Stuart painted this portrait in Washington not long before June 7, 1805. Jefferson was 62, and it was during that same year that he wrote one of the earliest descriptions of his architectural scheme for a university. He warned the directors of any new institution against "overbuilding themselves, by attempting a large house in the beginning, sufficient to contain the whole institution. Large houses are always ugly, inconven- ient, exposed to the accident of fire, and bad in cases of infection. A plain small house for the school and lodging of each professor is best, these connected by covered ways out of which the rooms of the students should open would be best. These may then be built only as they shall be wanting. In fact, an University should not be a house but a village."

Thomas Jefferson
at Seventy-three

7. Thomas Jefferson at seventy-three, 1816, by Bass Otis

Executed at Monticello in June, 1816, this painting is close in date to the beginning of Jefferson's architectural work for the University, work which he had started a short time before (see Illus. 8). Signs of age are already apparent in this likeness, about which Dr. William Thornton (see p. 18) said that "never was such injustice done to [Jefferson] except by sign painters."

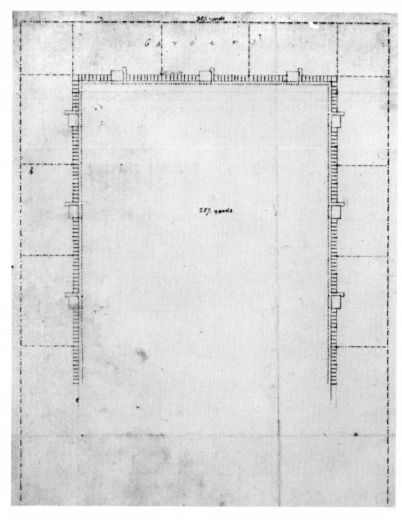

8. Early site plan for the University, *ca.* 1815

9. Early study for a pavilion and the adjacent students' rooms

Early Site Plan
for the University

This drawing, on the back of Illus. 9, shows nine pavilions arranged at equal distances about an open-ended square, with all pavilions identical. It lacks the major feature of the Rotunda. Jefferson said of his drawing that it was executed "2. or 3. years" before August, 1817, and Joseph C. Cabell speaks of it in a letter written late in 1815 (see p. 38).

Early Study for a Pavilion and
the Adjacent Students' Rooms

Notice especially the square brick piers used instead of columns and the simplicity of the pavilion itself. Jefferson himself points out on the drawing that "the pilasters [*i.e.*, piers] in front of the Pavilion are erroneously placed. The two outer should be opposite the corners & the inner should be equally distanced between them."

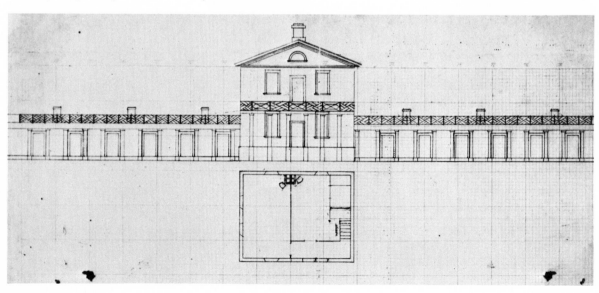

Latrobe's Suggestion
for a Rotunda

Benjamin Henry Latrobe (1764–
1820) had worked with Jefferson in Washington, D.C., and was
nearing the end of his appointment for rebuilding the Capitol
there when Jefferson requested his
ideas for the new College, as it
then was. Latrobe sent this
suggestion for a site plan. Jefferson was at once convinced by Latrobe's sketch of a dominant,
domical feature, adopted it whole-
heartedly, and retained it in his
scheme from then on. The con-
tours of the land purchased for
the new institution, however, had
caused Jefferson to abandon the
open-ended square shown in Illus.
8 and in Latrobe's letter for the
more rectangular Lawn, as executed. By August 3, 1817, the date
of Jefferson's reply to Latrobe,
building operations had started
on Pavilion VII.

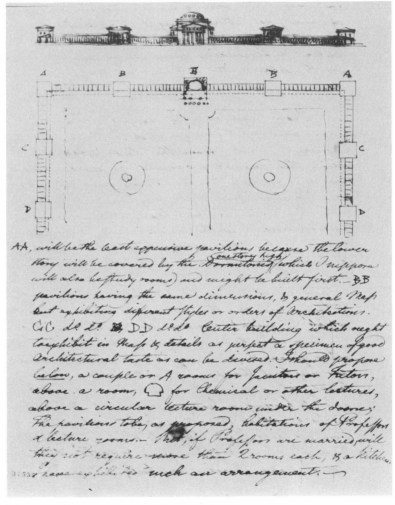

10.   Latrobe's suggestions for a Rotunda, 1817

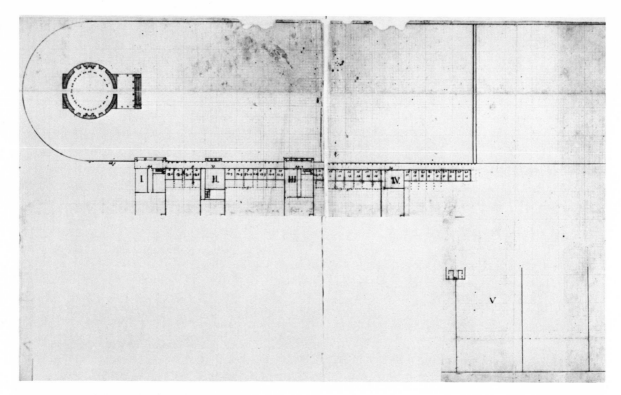

11. Unfinished study for the Lawn and ranges

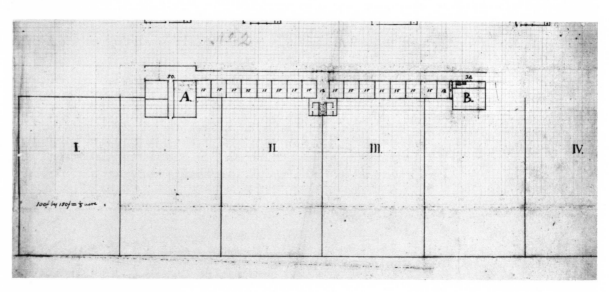

12. Rearrangement of the ranges

Plat Showing Location of
the Rotunda and
East and West Streets

In this drawing, almost certainly
by Jefferson and probably executed after the cutting of the pre-
vious study, the new concept of
the two streets parallel to the
ranges appears. There is also an
early suggestion of the serpentine
garden walls, although the pavilions and ranges are not outlined.

Unfinished Study for
the Lawn and Ranges

These two sheets, possibly drawn
by Jefferson as early as 1817, were
originally a single study of the
Lawn with West Range facing
the backs of the pavilions, while
the large gardens were to lie to the
west of the Range. The portion of
the sheet cut out, however, allowed Jefferson to study the feasi-
bility of facing the Range to the
west. Note that by the time this
drawing was made columns had
been substituted for piers on the
Lawn's covered way, that the pavilions were no longer identical,
and that the serpentine walls were
not yet suggested. The cutting of
the sheet and the reversal of the
position of the ranges was not
done until the spring of 1819
when Joseph C. Cabell (see p. 38)
suggested such a change. Jefferson said he thought "it a real improvement, and the greater as by
throwing the Hotels and addi-
tional dormitories on a back
street, it forms in fact the commencement of a regular town capable of being enlarged to any
extent which future circumstances
may call for." Unfortunately this
idea for future expansion was
never executed.

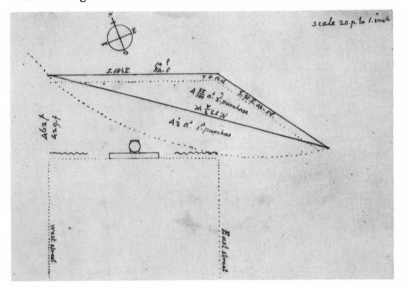

13. Plat showing location of the Rotunda and East and West Streets

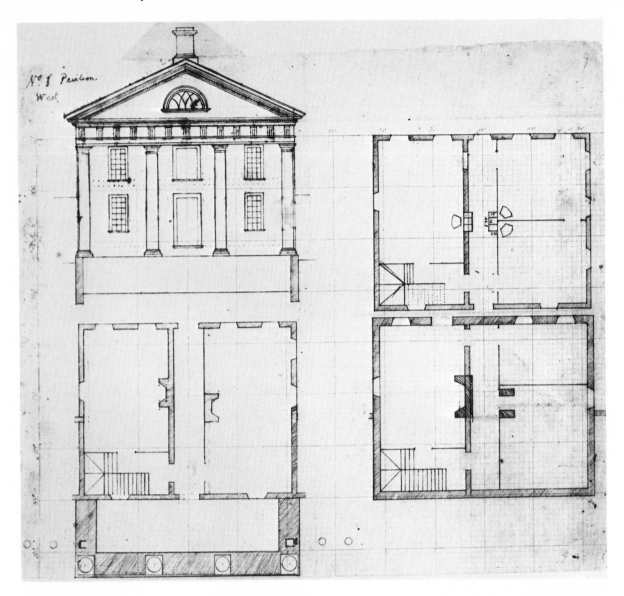

14. Pavilion I

The Five Pavilions on West Lawn

It is impossible to date Jefferson's drawings for West Lawn exactly. That for Pavilion VII, the first started, must have been executed between May 27, 1817, when Dr. William Thornton sent down his sketch of suggested pavilion fronts (see Illus. 18), and June 23–28, when construction had started. Pavilions III, V, and IX, the next to be started, were probably drawn sometime after October, 1817, while Pavilion I may not have been drawn until as late as July, 1819. It was not finished until 1822, but the other four were completed by September 30, 1821.

Dr. Thornton's suggestions for the pavilions were adapted schematically by Jefferson for Pavilion VII, but with striking differences in proportions and orders. The cornerstone for this pavilion was laid by President James Monroe on October 6, 1817, in the presence of former Presidents Jefferson and Madison. Later that same year, Latrobe's suggestions came down from Washington, but the drawings are now lost. We do know from Jefferson's letters that some of them showed "columns being of the height of both stories," a device which Jefferson used in Pavilions I, III, and V on West Lawn and in Pavilions II, IV, VIII, and X on East Lawn. In a letter to Latrobe, Jefferson also said that "having decided to build two more pavilions the ensuing season [Pavilions III and V], we shall certainly select their fronts from [Latrobe's drawings]. They will be Ionic and Corinthian." In addition, Latrobe's name is inscribed on the drawing for Pavilion IX in Jefferson's hand, a design which derives from the French architect Ledoux. Note that Pavilions III, V, and IX had parapets that have subsequently disappeared.

Jefferson derived the orders for these pavilions from Giacomo Leoni's 1721 London edition of Palladio's *Four Books of Architecture* and from the Paris 1766 edition of the French theorists Fréart de Chambray and Charles Errard's *Parallele de l'architecture antique*. The precedents for the orders on West Lawn are the Doric of the Baths of Diocletian from Chambray for Pavilion I; the Corinthian of Palladio for Pavilion III; the Ionic of Palladio for Pavilion V; the Doric of Palladio derived from an illustration in Chambray for Pavilion VII; and the Ionic of the Temple of Fortuna Virilis from Palladio for Pavilion IX.

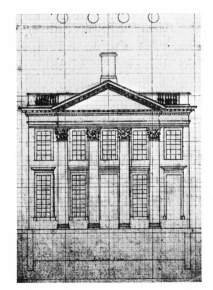

15. Pavilion III

16. Pavilion V

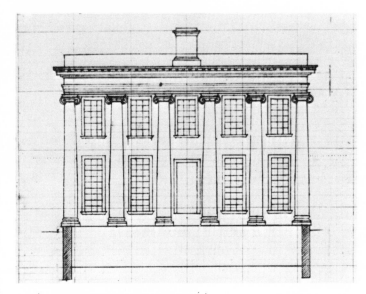

17. Pavilion VII

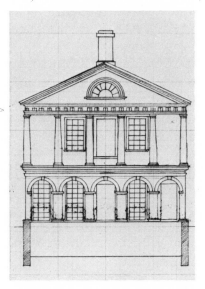

Façades for Pavilions
Suggested by Dr. Thornton

Dr. William Thornton (1759–1828), a man of many talents, had won the competition for the Capitol at Washington and was later head of the Patent Office. He knew Jefferson well and began his reply to Jefferson's request for aid with the designs for the University by saying "I will freely communicate my ideas," telling at great length what he thought might be improved in Jefferson's scheme. It is worth noting that his designs were only used once, and then only as a basis for Pavilion VII.

18. Façades for pavilions suggested by Dr. William Thornton

19. James Monroe

James Monroe

James Monroe (1758–1831) was the third of the Presidents of the United States to be intimately associated with the University. His studies at William and Mary were interrupted by the Revolution when he went into the army, fighting in many of the campaigns. By 1782 he was a member of the Virginia Assembly and from that time on held many political offices. He succeeded Madison as President in 1816 and the next year laid the cornerstone for Pavilion VII (see Illus. 17). At that time a visitor of Central College, he resigned before the University was chartered in 1819. After his presidency he served on the University's Board of Visitors from 1826 to 1831. Monroe, who lived in many residences during his lifetime, owned for a short period the house and land now called Monroe Hill (Illus. 69), a part of the University holdings.

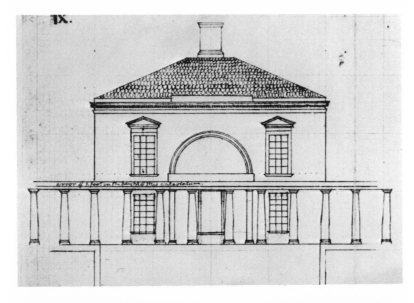

20. Pavilion IX

Thomas Jefferson
in 1819

Peter Cardelli modeled this bust
from life immediately after May
24, 1819, when Jefferson was seventy-six. No less a person than
John Quincy Adams had urged
Jefferson to give a sitting to
Cardelli, a sculptor who had
previously worked at carving orna-
ments on the Capitol at Washington. The signs of advancing age
are most apparent in this likeness,
made just before Jefferson prepared the drawings for East Lawn.
The photograph is of a twentieth-
century plaster cast of the original, now destroyed.

21. Thomas Jefferson, 1819, by Peter
Cardelli

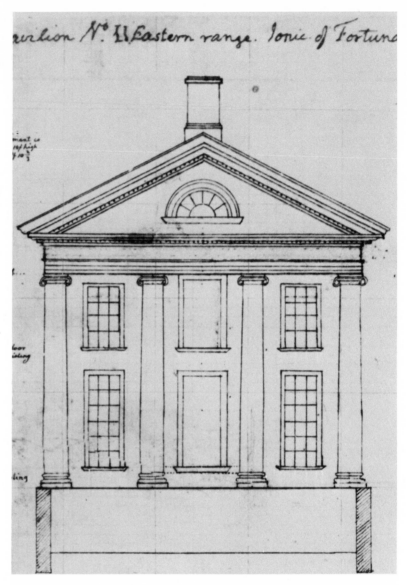

22. Pavilion II

The Five Pavilions
of East Lawn

Jefferson performed the remarkable feat of executing these five drawings in no more than fifteen days. He said on June 5, 1819, that he would not have the time to "turn to that business till the week after the ensuing one," but by June 27 he was able to speak of "the plans for the Eastern range of Pavilions which I have now prepared." Since Jefferson was seventy-six, this was indeed rapid work.

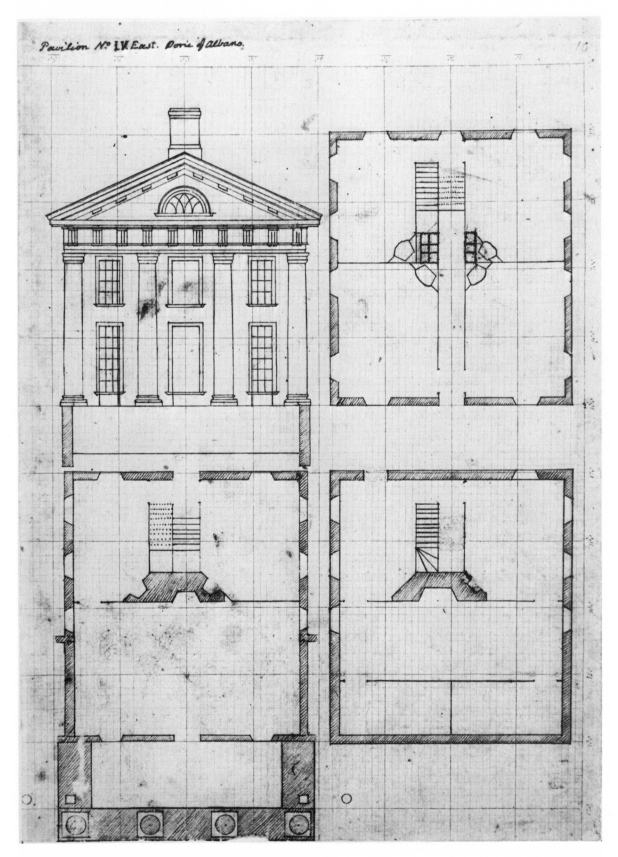

23. Pavilion IV

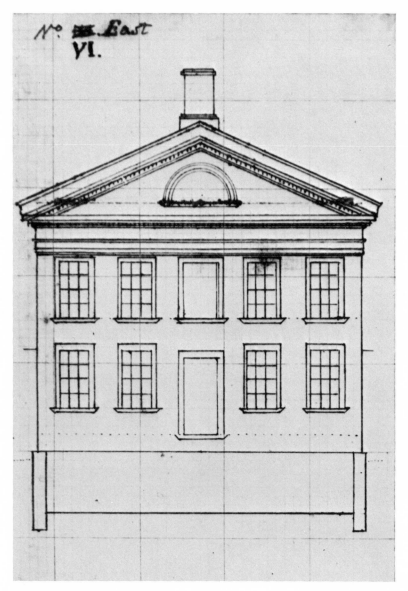

24. Pavilion VI

Of these buildings on East Lawn, only Pavilion VIII is acknowledged to have been suggested by Latrobe. On the specifications in his notebook for that pavilion Jefferson wrote "Latrobe's Lodge front," lodge being a word he sometimes used instead of the term pavilion. One should also note that Pavilions VIII and X had parapets that have subsequently disappeared. The columns for Pavilion VIII were originally freestanding, allowing daylight to fall into the entrance recess on either side of a catwalk from the second-floor door to the upper terrace.

The orders for East Lawn were derived from the Ionic of the Temple of Fortuna Virilis from Palladio for Pavilion II; the Doric of Albano from Chambray for Pavilion IV; the Ionic of the Theater of Marcellus from Chambray for Pavilion VI (for the entablature, since the pavilion is without columns); the Corinthian of Diocletian's Baths from Chambray for Pavilion VIII; and the Doric of the Theater of Marcellus from Chambray for Pavilion X, while its now missing parapet was derived from that of the Temple of Nerva Trajan as illustrated in Palladio.

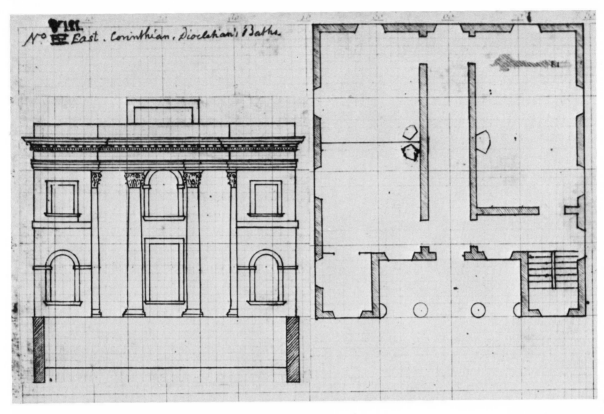

25.   Pavilion VIII

26.   Pavilion X

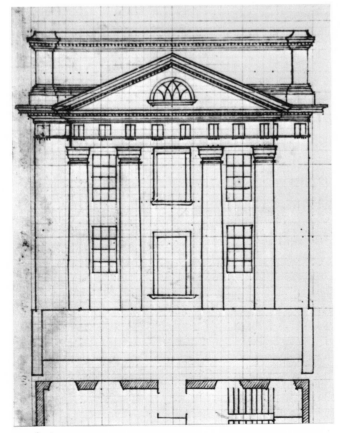

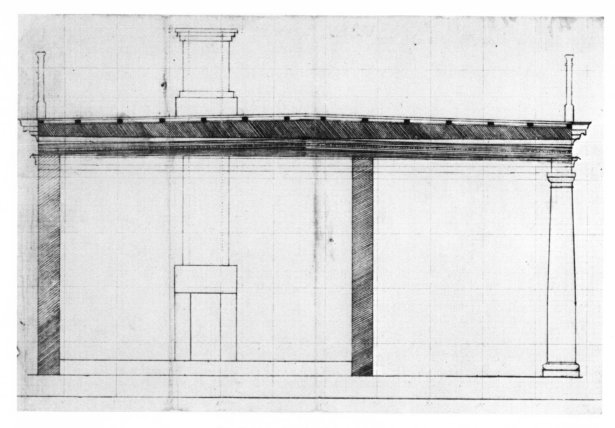

27.   Section of student's room on Lawn

28.   Portion of colonnade on Lawn

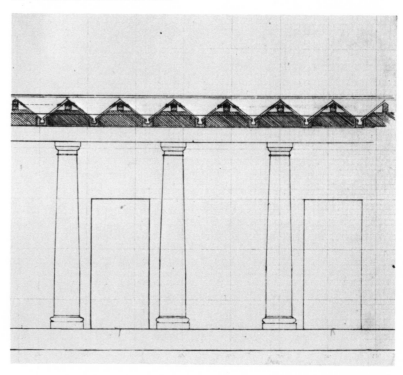

Details of the
Lawn

These three drawings by Jefferson, perhaps executed as early as 1817, show several features of the University that cannot be seen today. First, the three drawings of columns (the Tuscan order derived from Leoni's Palladio) do not have the "milk-bottle" shape that is sometimes present in the existing columns and that is undoubtedly the result of inferior workmanship. Secondly, Illus. 27 and 28 clearly outline the flattened roof that these dormitories originally had, sections of which still exist beneath the ridge roof visible today, and the heavy wooden railings that had crowned the flat roof (that served as a terrace or walk between the second floors of the pavilions) and that were replaced by the present delicate and partially Gothic iron railings. The Jeffersonian term for this roof system was "rooflets." Finally Illus. 27 gives an idea of the austerity of the students' rooms themselves, the wall crowned with the exterior architrave carried inside, and the very simple fireplaces.

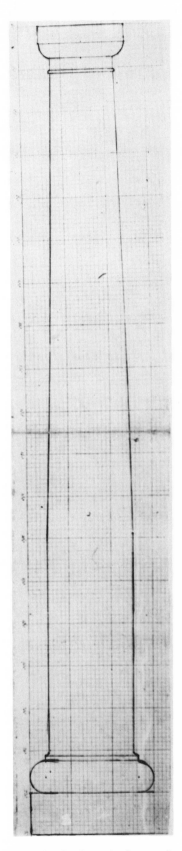

29. Study of column for Lawn colonnade

Multiple-Storied Dormitories

In the spring of 1819 Jefferson's scheme for East and West Range was attacked by some members of his Board of Visitors, who, although they thought Jefferson's design "beautiful and magnificent," felt that multistory buildings would serve the students' needs both better and more economically. This drawing, annotated by and possibly drawn by Jefferson—its authorship is uncertain although its attribution to Gen. Cocke (see p. 39) is disproved since it is not on the "graduated paper" he said he used in his studies of multistory dormitories sent to Jefferson—shows by its inferior design the wisdom of retaining the original scheme.

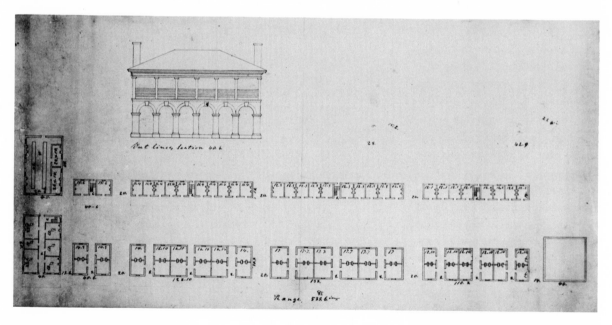

30. Scheme for multiple-storied dormitories

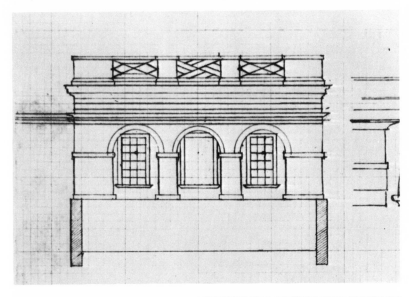

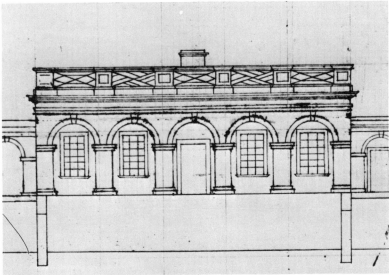

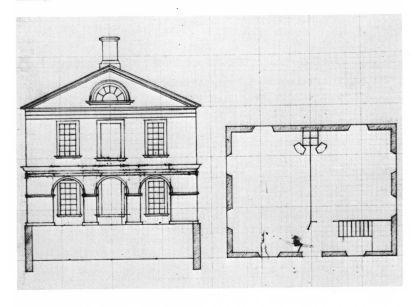

The Three Hotels for East Range

Jefferson's argument for retaining his original scheme for the ranges, an argument which apparently convinced the Board, was that they had been a part of the plan when it was adopted, first by the Rockfish Gap Commission and secondly by the Legislature. Because of its official standing, he felt that it would be extremely difficult to change to another form.

These three drawings were made by Jefferson about May, 1820. Note that the roofs shown in Illus. 31 and 32 are flat and that they are surmounted by what Jefferson termed a "Chinese railing." Illus. 32 is the best representation of the range arcades and dormitories that has survived. They, too, had flat roofs while their cornice was topped by a very low parapet. Illus. 33 shows the only two-story hotel at the University, but it, like the other two on East Range, has been changed radically over the years. All three hotels were finished in 1822.

31. Northeast Hotel
32. Center Hotel
33. Southeast Hotel

The Three Hotels
on West Range

Although there is a fragmentary
Jeffersonian drawing of the hotel
shown as Illus. 35, no complete
drawing by him of either Illus. 34
or Illus. 35 is known to exist. The
two drawings of these hotels reproduced here are probably by his
granddaughter, Cornelia Jefferson
Randolph. They may be dated *ca.*
1820. Illus. 36, dating before
1821, was drawn by Jefferson and
shows the hotel as a flat-roofed
building capped by a Chinese railing. These buildings, too, were finished by 1822. All of them have
undergone considerable changes,
although the northwest hotel
(Illus. 34) has now been restored
to its original form.

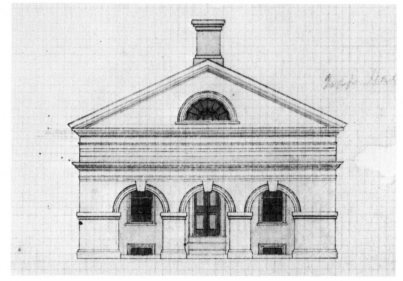

34. Northwest Hotel
35. Center Hotel
36. Southwest Hotel

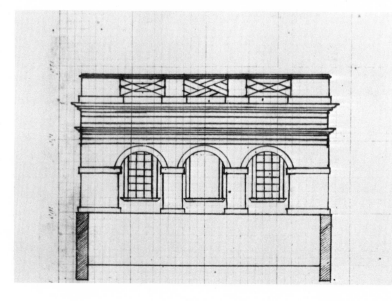

Bird's-Eye View of
the University

This curious drawing, thought to
be by Jefferson with the shading
by his granddaughter, shows the
University with its original roof
forms intact, although it omits the
Rotunda. It probably dates from
1820. One scholar has pointed out
that the perspective method, one
of "parallel perspective with the
vanishing point far to one side,"
was derived by Jefferson from his
copy of the splendid folio set of
John Joshua Kirby's *The Perspective of Architecture* (London,
1761).

37. Bird's-eye view of the University

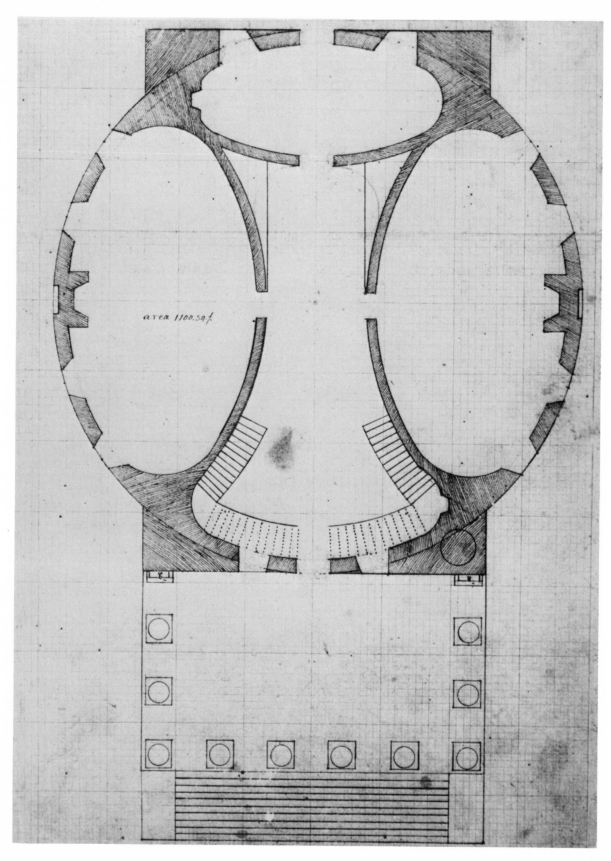

area 1100.sq.f.

38.   First-floor plan, the Rotunda

The Rotunda

These drawings of the Rotunda (Illus. 38, 39, 40, and 41) may probably be dated before March 29, 1821, when the Proctor made a careful estimate of its cost. They were certainly drawn before April 2, 1821, when they were approved by the Board of Visitors. The plans in Illus. 38 and 39 were originally parts of a single folded sheet but are now separate. The specifications, also in Jefferson's hand, on the back of that sheet began "Rotunda reduced to the proportions of the Pantheon and accommodated to the purposes of a Library for the University with rooms for drawing, music, examinations and other accessory purposes. The diameter of the building 77. feet, being ½ that of the Pantheon, consequently ¼ it's area, & ⅛ it's volume." For his information about the Pantheon, Jefferson drew on Leoni's 1721 edition of Palladio, in which there were no less than eleven plates illustrating it.

Notice that there was no north portico at this time. The ground-floor plan repeated that of the first floor without the portico, of course, while one ascended eventually into the very beautiful Library Room, the topmost of the original three floors, with its coupled columns of the Composite order, also derived from the Leoni *Palladio*. This colonnade, in turn, supported two balconies, which were to be used for book storage. Although the first and second floor were supported by brick partitions, there were no true vaults in the building. The *wooden* dome was a portion of a true sphere in the Library Room, and Jefferson

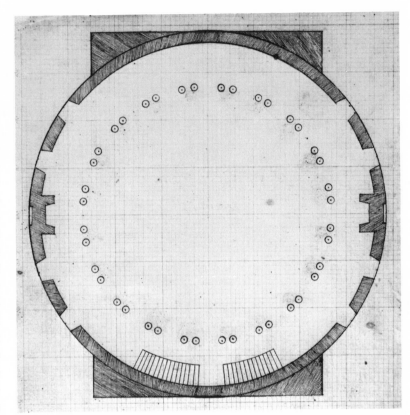

39. Second-floor plan (the Library floor), the Rotunda

40. South elevation, the Rotunda

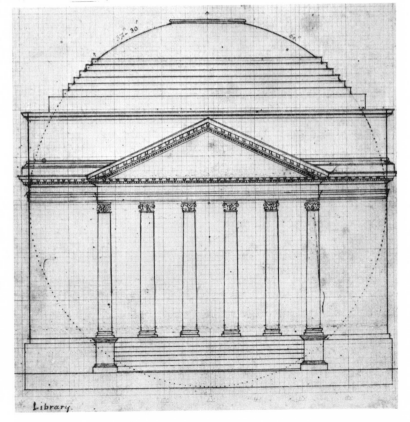

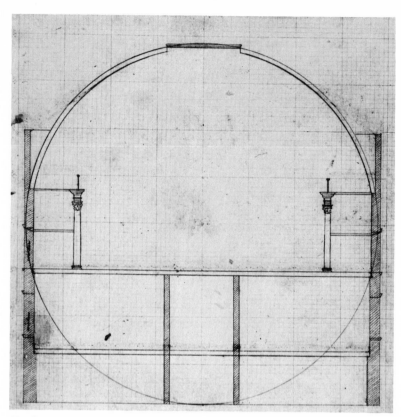

41. Section, the Rotunda

had meant for it to be painted in a representation of the constellations.

The arcades for the Gymnasia were the wings on either side of the Rotunda. The drawing (Illus. 42) has notes on the reverse side in Jefferson's hand dated April 26, 1824. These arcades completed the covered walkway around the Lawn, gave sheltered but outdoor exercise space, and, since their floor was at the level of the basement of the Rotunda, only extended a few feet above the Lawn on their south side.

42. Arcades for the Gymnasia, the Rotunda

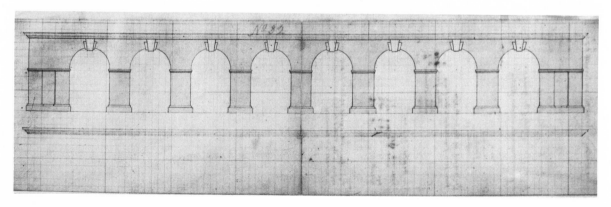

43. View of the Lawn from the south

View of the Lawn
from the South

In this elevational drawing of the Lawn from the south, probably by Cornelia Jefferson Randolph and dating from about 1820, we can best see Jefferson's original conception of the University. The neoclassicism of the parapeted Pavilions IX and X, the proportions of the original railings, and the cylindrical solidity of the Rotunda show us the purity of the architectural conception of its creator. The loss of the first railings and first roof forms obscures that aspect at present. Notice the steps at the base of the Rotunda dome and the flat skylight that caps it, both features which are no longer extant.

The Marquis de Lafayette

The Marquis de Lafayette was one of the University's early distinguished visitors, arriving in Charlottesville during his triumphal tour of the United States in 1824, before the University was finished. Jefferson wrote on October 12, 1824, that Lafayette was "to visit Montpelier and Monticello within about three weeks, and to accept a public dinner in our University. The Rotunda is sufficiently advanced to receive him." At the dinner itself, Jefferson, in response to a toast to himself, stated that he would "cheerfully and zealously" make any possible contribution to the advance of the institution.

44.   The Marquis de Lafayette, 1826, by
        Samuel F. B. Morse

The Anatomical Theater

This drawing for the Anatomical Theater, made by Jefferson before March 4, 1825, demonstrates Jefferson's functionalism, especially in his placement of the lunetted windows above eye level so that the interior would have light without the possibility of people seeing in from the outside and in the use of a skylight over the center of the operating theater. The Anatomical Theater is the only University building designed by Jefferson to have been demolished. Though much altered, it survived until 1938, when it was torn down to make way for Alderman Library. Since construction did not begin on it until 1826, it was one of the last of the Jeffersonian buildings to be started, and was unfinished at the time of Jefferson's death.

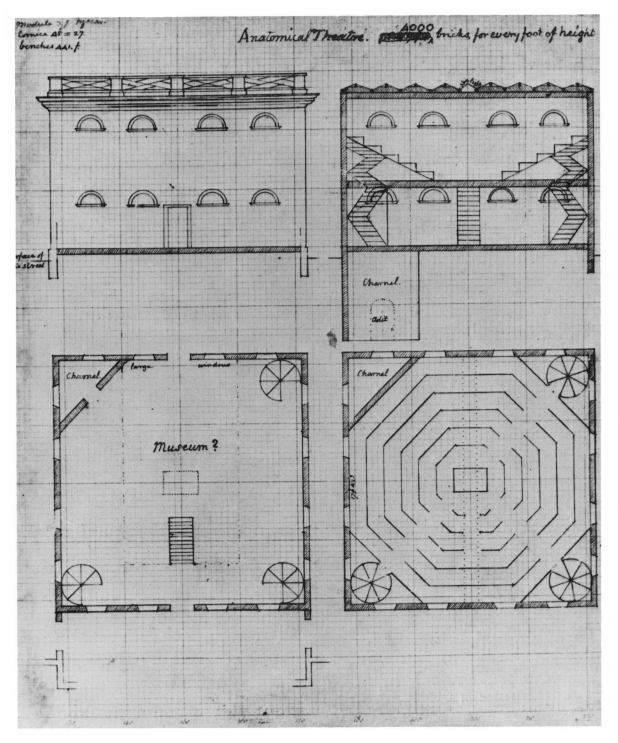

45. The Anatomical Theater

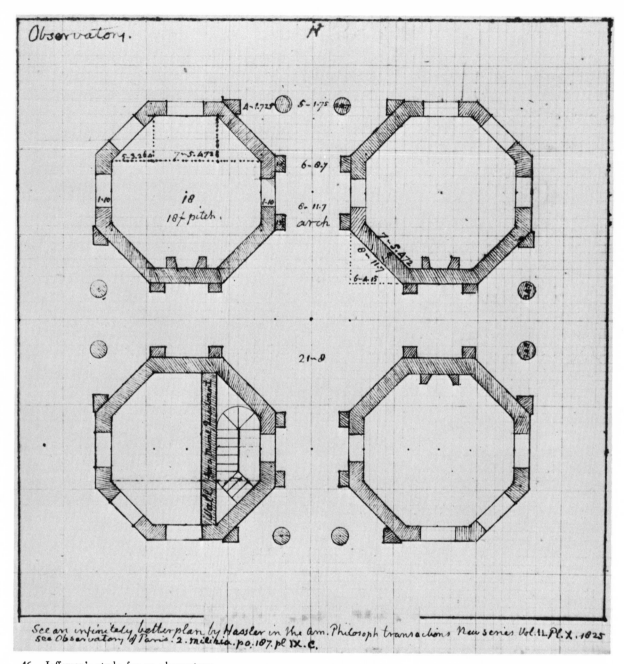

46. Jefferson's study for an observatory

Study for an Observatory

Jefferson made two studies for an observatory, which he felt should be an integral part of the new University. The drawings were probably done in 1825. His notes on the one reproduced here show his habit of consulting references to reinforce his architectural thinking. In his notes for an observatory he specifies that "it be so solid" that it is "not liable to tremble," that it open "in every direction," that it have "one position perfectly solid," and that "as to the height of the building, the less the solider." This proposed building was never erected, although not long after the University opened, it did have an observatory housed in a remodeled building.

The First Board of Visitors

Thomas Jefferson
in 1825

On October 15, 1825, Jefferson certified that "Mr. Browere has this day made a mould in Plaister composition, from my person for the purpose of making a portrait Bust and Statue for his contemplated National Gallery." On October 19 Madison said that this portrait "has been submitted to our inspection and appears to be a faithful likeness." Browere's scheme for a "National Gallery" failed, but the cast he made from his life mask of Jefferson has survived. Although the infirmities of age are plainly seen in this portrait, one must remember that Jefferson, as Rector of the Board of Visitors, kept a firm hand on the affairs of the new University until his death on July 4, 1826.

47. Thomas Jefferson, 1825, by John Henri Isaac Browere

48. Joseph Carrington Cabell, by Louis Mathieu Didier Guillaume

James Breckenridge

James Breckenridge (1763–1846) was born at Fincastle, Botetourt County, and educated at William and Mary, graduating in 1785. He entered the practice of law in 1787 at Fincastle and continued there throughout his life. His political life brought him frequent membership in the Virginia General Assembly and eventually led to a seat in the House of Representatives in Washington from 1809 to 1817. During the War of 1812 he rose to the rank of general and had as one of his aides Chapman Johnson. They were both later members of the Board of Visitors of the University, Breckenridge serving from 1819 to 1833.

No portrait of Breckenridge has been found.

Joseph Carrington Cabell

Joseph Carrington Cabell (1778–1856) was born at Warminster on the James. He was educated there, at private schools in Albemarle County, at Hampden-Sidney College, and at William and Mary, from which he graduated in 1798. He studied law under St. George Tucker, whose stepdaughter he later married. Cabell completed his studies in Europe, where he met both Robert Fulton and Washington Irving, visited Edward Jenner, spent a winter studying botany at Montpellier, France, and toured many of the European universities. By 1808 Cabell was a member of Virginia's House of Delegates, and he was a state senator from 1810 to 1829. His principal public interests were internal improvements, agriculture, and education. This last interest brought him the offices of trustee of the Charlottesville Ladies Academy, member of the Rockfish Gap Commission, and visitor of the University of Virginia, 1819–1856. He was Rector of the University twice, first from 1834–1836 and secondly from 1845–1856.

Of the early days of the institution at Charlottesville he wrote in 1815 "notwithstanding my unabated regard for William and Mary, I shall do everything in my power to give success to Mr. Jefferson's scheme of a college now pending before the Assembly. The more the better. He has drafted a beautiful scheme of a college at Charlottesville." He achieved these aims during his long service in the State Senate.

The portrait reproduced here was painted at the expense of the faculty of the University, who had ordered it on November 15, 1856, "to give expression to their regard and their grateful remembrance of his uniform courtesy and kindness towards them."

49. John Hartwell Cocke, by William James Hubbard

50. Chapman Johnson, by James W. Ford

John Hartwell Cocke

Chapman Johnson

John Hartwell Cocke (1780–1866) was born in Surry County and educated at William and Mary, from which he received his degree in 1798. During the War of 1812 he served on the Chickahominy River and in the defense of Richmond and rose to the rank of brigadier general. Jefferson asked the governor to appoint Cocke to the Board of Visitors, and he served for no less than thirty-three years. During his first years as a Visitor he also served with Jefferson as the committee of superintendence and helped with the supervision of construction at the University. After Jefferson's death, Cocke, who had established Bremo Academy, wanted to buy Monticello in order to use it for a school modeled after the German gymnasium. This scheme failed. Cocke, whose home was at Bremo, was vice president of the American Temperance Society and of the American Colonization Society and established schools for Negroes both at Bremo and on his land in Mississippi, sending the graduates of this latter school to Liberia.

The portrait reproduced here is the gift to the University of Virginia of Mrs. Mazyck Wilson Shields.

Chapman Johnson (1779–1849), born in Louisa County, was educated at William and Mary, where he studied law under St. George Tucker, graduating in 1802. He practiced law first at Staunton, became well known for his ability, and moved to Richmond in 1829. He was a captain of a volunteer company in the War of 1812, later becoming an aide to Gen. James Breckenridge; a member of the Board of Visitors of the University of Virginia, 1819–1845; and a state senator, 1815–1831.

Ford's portrait of Johnson was the gift to the University of Mr. Paul E. Manheim in 1964.

James Madison

James Madison (1751–1836), born in Port Conway, Virginia, was educated at Princeton, from which he received his bachelor's degree in 1771. His long career of legislative service began at the state convention in 1776 which called for Independence, and included membership in the Continental Congress in 1780–83, the Virginia General Assembly, and the U.S. House of Representatives, as well as an active role in the creation of the Federal Constitution of 1787.

In 1805 Jefferson called him to Washington to be Secretary of State, after which he served two terms as President, 1808–1812 and 1812–1816. In 1817 he returned to Montpelier in Orange County and soon began serving on the Board of Visitors of the new University, an appointment he kept until 1834, succeeding Jefferson as Rector in 1826. Although he willed his library to the University, due to technicalities only some 2,000 volumes were received, and of these most were destroyed in the 1895 fire.

51. James Madison. Engraving after the original portrait by Gilbert Stuart

Beginning Splendor

1825–1861

52. View of the Lawn, 1837

View of the Lawn, 1837

This romanticized view of the Lawn was a German version published in a work called *Meyer's Universum* in 1837. It was engraved by T. Poppel, who imaginatively added a series of statues to the Rotunda terraces and cupola (itself a great exaggeration), flattened the Lawn, and changed the proportions of many of the pavilions. His print does show, however, the parapeted pavilions and the flat roofs of the students' rooms.

The First Faculty

Francis Walker Gilmer

After the University's buildings were assured and well under way, the next task was that of assembling a faculty of the highest available quality. Since it soon became apparent that enough well-trained teachers were not to be found in this country, Jefferson and the Board of Visitors sent 34-year-old Francis Walker Gilmer (1790–1826) to England to recruit a faculty. Gilmer, who had been educated at Georgetown College and William and Mary and had studied law under William Wirt of Richmond, had been elected to the chair of law at the University.

Although he was in delicate health at the time he sailed to England on May 8, 1824, on the *Cortez*, he not only hired several members of the new faculty, the eldest of whom was 28 and the youngest 24, but he purchased $6,000 worth of scientific instruments and found time to copy John Smith's *History of Virginia* for publication in this country.

He left England on October 5, 1825, but when he reached Charlottesville he was too ill to take up his post, which was filled by John Tayloe Lomax (see p. 45). He died on February 25, 1826, at Farmington. Chapman Johnson was not very sympathetic to poor Gilmer's illness, for he wrote him once, "Make up your mind to get well or to go to heaven without another murmur or complaining word."

Nevertheless, an enormous burden of trust was placed on Gil-

53. Francis Walker Gilmer

mer's shoulders by Jefferson when he asked him to choose members of the faculty, and Jefferson's own resilience of mind is demonstrated once more in his choice of so young a man as Gilmer for this task and his acceptance of the very young men Gilmer brought back.

The portrait of Gilmer by an unknown painter was the gift to the University of his niece, Mrs. Lucy A. Minor, in 1881.

George Blaetterman

Charles Bonnycastle

Robley Dunglison

George Blaetterman, whose birth and death dates are not known, was a German who had emigrated to London. Having been recommended to Jefferson in 1821 by both George Ticknor and General Preston, he applied directly in 1823 and was accepted after Richard Rush, the American Minister to London, examined his qualifications and character. Blaetterman was the professor of modern languages and offered French, Spanish, Italian, German, and Anglo-Saxon and was also able to teach Danish, Swedish, Portuguese, and "Hollandish," as the University's catalogue said.

Rush's estimate of his knowledge was right, but that of his character was wrong, for Blaetterman was asked to resign his chair after beating his wife in public. He taught for two more years, however, until 1840, when he went to Limestone, a nearby farm where he was later found dead in the snow of a fit of apoplexy. No portrait of Blaetterman has been found.

Charles Bonnycastle (1796–1840) was the son of John Bonnycastle, professor of mathematics at the Royal Military Institute, Woolwich, where Charles was educated. He was brought here as professor of natural philosophy and introduced the latest methods of teaching, putting the University far ahead of contemporary American schools.

Although Bonnycastle married a Miss Tutt of Loudoun County, and had three children, he was so shy he would climb over fences or walk through mud in order to avoid a student. His death was attributed to his habit of never taking exercise. In spite of his shyness, however, he was chairman of the faculty from 1833 to 1835, and the faculty purchased Ford's painting from the artist in 1837 and presented it to the University.

Robley Dunglison (1798–1869), born at Keswick, Cumberland, was educated in medicine in London and Erlanger, Germany. In London he not only practiced medicine but became editor of the *London Medical Repository* and the *Medical Intelligencer*. His literary interest continued in this country, where he established the *Virginia Literary Museum and Journal of Belles-Letters, Arts and Sciences* (1828) and later worked on many translations.

He came to the University of Virginia as professor of medicine and was the first secretary to the faculty and its chairman in 1826 and again in 1828 to 1830. In 1833 he left Charlottesville for the University of Maryland in Baltimore, and subsequently went to the Jefferson Medical College in Philadelphia where he died after a long and honored life. When his brain was examined after his death it was found to weigh five ounces more than that of the average English male.

The portrait reproduced was a gift to the University from his son, Richard J. Dunglison.

John Patton Emmet

Thomas Hewitt Key

John Tayloe Lomax

John Patton Emmet (1796–1842) was born in Ireland but came to this country in 1804. He was educated in Flatbush and at West Point, where he soon became acting assistant professor of mathematics. He left West Point, however, in 1817 and went to Naples because of his health. There he studied music, sculpture, and art and became fluent in ancient and modern languages. On his return to New York he trained as a physician, earning his M.D. in 1822. In Charleston, S.C., where he lived between 1822 and 1825, his lectures on chemistry became so famous that he was offered the chair of natural history at the University of Virginia.

Emmet, who was fond of animals, kept a small zoo in his pavilion, but his bride (Mary Byrd Tucker, the niece of George Tucker) had it removed and went so far as to have Emmet's tame bear killed and served as a "rare dish." Later the Emmets moved to Morea, now owned by the University, where he carried on his horticultural experiments and introduced *Pyracantha* to this area.

Thomas Hewitt Key (1799–1875), born in London the son of a physician, was educated at Buntingford Grammar School in Hertfordshire, at St. John's College, Cambridge, then Trinity College, Cambridge (B.A., 1821; M.A., 1824), and earned his M.D. at Guy's Hospital, London.

He came to the University of Virginia in 1825 as professor of mathematics but returned to the University of London in 1827 as professor of Latin, being succeeded in Charlottesville by Bonnycastle, who left the chair of natural philosophy. Key was one of the founders of the London Library, a fellow of the Royal Society, and a member of the Society for the Diffusion of Useful Knowledge.

John Tayloe Lomax (1781–1862) was born at Port Tobago, Caroline County. He was the only native Virginian on the original faculty. He had been educated at St. John's College, Annapolis, obtaining his degree at sixteen. Before his appointment as professor of law at the University (1826) he had been practicing law and conducting a small law school in Fredericksburg. He resigned his professorship in 1830 to accept a judgeship of the circuit court. He wrote the *Digest of the Laws of Real Property* (3 vols.; Philadelphia, 1839), which was used as a text by the University.

59. George Long
60. George Tucker

George Long

George Tucker

George Long (1800–1879) was the eldest son of James Long, a merchant in Poulton. He was educated at Macclesfield Grammar School and Trinity College, Cambridge, where he earned his B.A. in 1822, having been a contemporary of Macaulay. He was called to the University of Virginia as professor of ancient languages but stayed only until 1828, when he became professor of Greek at the University of London. In Charlottesville he married the daughter of Mr. Gay, the keeper of the southernmost hotel in West Range.

At the University of London he later succeeded Key as the professor of Latin and became a well-known writer and editor, working with the *Quarterly Journal of Education* and the *Penny Cyclopaedia,* both published by the Society for the Diffusion of Useful Knowledge, a lecturer on jurisprudence in the Inner Temple, a Fellow of Brighton College, and a founder of the Royal Geographical Society.

George Tucker (1775–1861) was born on Bermuda. At the age of 20 he came to William and Mary, where his cousin St. George Tucker was teaching law and where he himself studied law. Although he returned to Bermuda after completing his studies, he came back to this country in 1800, joined the Richmond bar in that year, and married Maria Carter, the great-niece of George Washington, in 1802. He eventually settled in Lynchburg, where he was elected to two terms in the House of Representatives after 1818.

Madison recommended him for the chair of moral philosophy at the University because of a volume of essays he had written. Tucker accepted the appointment, taking the chair at the age of fifty. He was chairman of the faculty in 1825, 1828, and from 1832 to 1833, but he resigned his post in 1845 and, removing to Philadelphia, gave the rest of his life to literature.

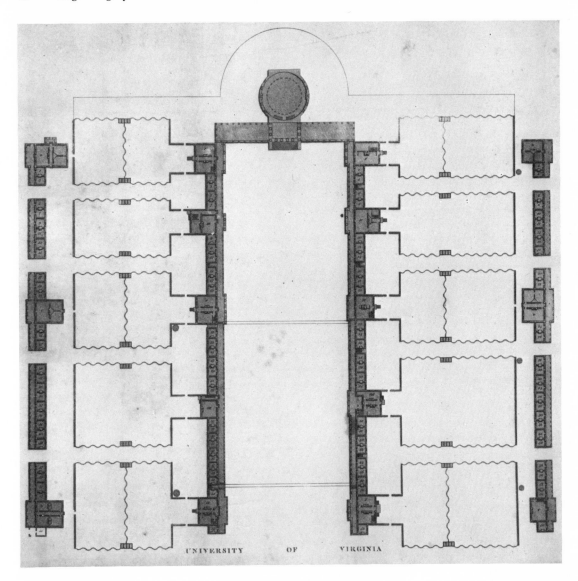

The Maverick Plan

61. The Maverick Plan, by Peter Maverick

Peter Maverick, the New York engraver, executed his first ground plan of the University of Virginia sometime after March 22, 1822, from a drawing by Jefferson (now in the Virginia State Library) that had been brought to him at that time by William Coffee, the ornamentist, when he returned to New York from Monticello. Archaeological investigation during the spring of 1950 showed that the engraving was an accurate representation, especially of the location of the garden walls, rather than a generalized diagram.

A second edition of the Maverick Plan was delivered March 3, 1825, an edition which had the dormitory rooms numbered, and which is reproduced here. Note the cisterns and the lack of gates between the gardens for the professors and those for the students. These plans were sent to prospective students for a fee.

EXPLANATIONS,

OF THE GROUND PLAN OF THE UNIVERSITY OF VIRGINIA.

Nos. I, II, III. IV, V, VI, VII, VIII, IX, X, are Pavilions, of two stories each, for the residence of the Professors separately, with each a lecturing room, and generally four rooms of accommodation for the family—a back yard and garden. The offices are below.

The small apartments numbered 1, to 55, filling the intervals between the Pavilions, are Dormitories of a single story, for two students each ; all opening into a colonnade, along the whole range of 600 feet in length. These Dormitories have a flat roof, in the level of the upper floor of the Pavilions, which, through the Porticos, gives a private walk and communication to the families inhabiting the Pavilions.

A, B, C, D, E, F, are Hotels, to be let to housekeepers for dieting the students. The small intervening apartments, numbered 1 to 56, are Dormitories, as those of the two middle rows, all opening into arcades, continued along the whole range, 600 feet in length each, These Hotels have their offices below, with each a back-yard and garden, separated by cross-streets of communication with the Pavilions.

The ground between the two middle rows, in front and back of the Rotunda, is an open lawn looking S. S. E. 200 feet wide, and at present 900 feet in length, left open at one end for a continuation of the buildings indefinitely.

The ROTUNDA, filling up the Northernmost end of the ground is 77 feet in diameter, and in height, crowned by a Dome of 120 deg. of the sphere. The lower floor has large rooms for religious worship, for public examinations, and other associated purposes. The upper floor is a single room for a Library, canopied by the Dome and it's sky-light.

The Rotunda is connected with the two rows of Pavilions by a Terras on each side of the height of its Basement, and breadth of the flank of it's Portico; below the Terras is a space for gymnastick exercises, and a covered way uniting those of the two colonnades, and affording a sheltered passage round three sides of the lawn, 1400 feet in extent.

Within the back-yards are cisterns of fountain water, brought in pipes from a neighbouring mountain.

☞ *Plans of the University of Virginia, can be had by applying to the Proctor, at 50 cents each, and the Report of the Commissioners at 12 1-2 cents.*

62.   Explanations of the ground plan of the University of Virginia

63.   A student in 1853, by Porte Crayon

Explanations of the Ground Plan of the University of Virginia

When the second edition of the Maverick engraving of the ground plan of the University was delivered, Jefferson had this explanation of it printed for those sending in for information. This Jeffersonian description is one of the best to have survived of the original group of University buildings, and many of the terms that are still in use today may be traced to this statement.

A Student in the 1850's

The University opened its classes on March 7, 1825, with sixty-eight students. They were supposed to be self-governing, but by October, 1825, rioting and disorder became so bad that a full assembly of the students, the faculty, the Board of Visitors, and Jefferson, the Rector, was held. As a result the faculty was given enormous power over the students, who were put into uniforms and were not allowed to have even "a little chicken supper" in their rooms without the Proctor's consent. Riots occurred again in 1831 over uniforms and sporadically until 1839, when the chairman of the faculty was publicly horsewhipped, and 1840, when Professor John A. G. Davis was shot dead by a masked student. The establishment of the honor system in 1842 seems to have been the turning point in this long war between students and faculty.

In contrast to today's system, matriculation was unbelievably easy at this time. A student has left a record of enrolling in 1845—"I went at once to the

Proctor's office in the building now occupied by Washington Hall. The Proctor handed us a copy of the Laws of the institution, quite a thick pamphlet, and a pen to enter our name, age, etc., in the matriculation book."

The woodcut illustration of a University student is somewhat later than this, for it is taken from a drawing by Porte Crayon (David Hunter Strother) that he made during a visit to Charlottesville in 1853. After saying that the University "has a very pleasing and pretty effect but the buildings are too low, and the architecture wants finish," the artist goes on to point out that although "it was not eminently successful in its early years . . . it seems to be taking the position that it should have attained long ago, and its present catalogue shows over five hundred students."

Duties for Dormitory Servants

The list of duties for the dormitory servants, made up by the faculty in 1842, shows that neither servants nor students had a particularly easy time during their residence at the University.

64. Duties for dormitory servants, 1842

A Hunter, near the University

This charming, primitive picture, of uncertain date and uncertain origin, emphasizes the rural character of the University's grounds during the early years of its existence. Although there may be some poetic license in this bucolic view from the vicinity of Vinegar Hill, it is also interesting to see that the architecture of the Lawn dominated the landscape in such a way. The drawing can be dated before 1853, since the Annex had not yet been built.

Edgar Allan Poe

Of all the early students at the University, Edgar Allan Poe is probably the most famous. He matriculated February 14, 1826, and stayed for a complete session, that is until December 15 of that same year, working in the schools of ancient and modern languages. Although he lived first on West Lawn, he soon moved to West Range, and it is thought, on the recollections of former college mates, that Room 13 on West Range was his.

Poe wrote his foster father that in addition to $15.00 paid in advance for his room he had paid "$12 more for a bed and $12 more for room furniture." When the room was refurnished in 1942 under the direction of Edmund S. Campbell, furniture of Poe's time was purchased for the amount equivalent to twenty-four of the 1826 dollars.

In 1956 the Poe Room was given its present aspect, and in 1958 A. Churchill Young, Jr., gave the room the original small

65. A hunter, with the University in the background

66. Edgar Allan Poe, by George Julian Zolnay

67. Entrance to Poe Room

bed Poe slept in at his foster parents' home in Richmond. The bronze tablet over the door was a gift of Miss Bangs. It reads "Domus Parva Magni Poetae."

The bronze portrait, by George Julian Zolnay was unveiled in Cabell Hall on the fiftieth anniversary of Poe's death, October 7, 1899. The portrait was given to the University by the Poe Memorial Association, and the principal address at its dedication was given by Hamilton W. Makie.

68. Poe Room

69. Monroe Hill

Monroe Hill

Among the many existing buildings that came into the hands of the University with its purchase of land from John M. Perry in 1817 was Monroe Hill, so called because James Monroe built the first portion of the house there in 1790 and lived there until 1799. He sold it to John Nicholas in 1805, and Nicholas sold it to Perry in 1814.

Although Jefferson had hoped to convert the house into an observatory after his plan for a new one had been abandoned (see p. 36), the second plan was also abandoned, and the house was turned over to the Proctor for many years. Monroe Hill was enlarged to its present state at various dates, twelve dormitories were added in 1848, and at one time the State Scholars, students attending the University on grants from the Commonwealth, dined there.

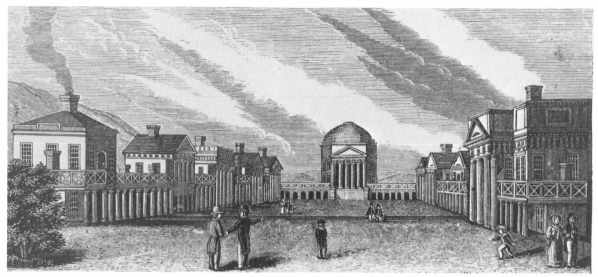

70. University of Virginia, *ca.* 1845

University of Virginia, *ca.* 1845

This woodcut view of the University, taken from Howe's *History of Virginia* (1845), shows the Lawn before change had set in. But the artist's medium and his lack of feeling for proportion have transformed Jefferson's creation into a heavy and awkward composition.

The University
from the East, 1850

This lithograph by P. S. Duval was published in 1850 in an *Autograph Album of the University*. It shows the walk (road ?) to East Street, the fence by the road alongside East Range, and the curious weather vane on top of the Rotunda's cupola. The cupola itself had been added by Gen. Cocke (see p. 39) after Jefferson's death. The gilded weather vane, supposedly in the shape of a quill pen (as

one alumnus remembered it), crowned the cupola, the quill being eight to ten feet long. The quill is said to have been removed *ca.* 1859–60 by William Pratt (see p. 62). On the other hand another alumnus, reminiscencing about 1890 of his time as a student just before the Civil War, thought the weather vane was an arrow, for he says "the cupola, rod and arrow were all removed" after he and some other students had attached a Confederate flag to it.

71. The University from the east, 1850

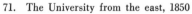

View of the University
from the East, 1853

Only three years after Illus. 71 was published the aspect of the University was radically altered by the addition to the north side of the Rotunda of the New Hall, or the Annex as it is more familiarly known. This view of the new building is dated October, 1853, when the artist was in Charlottesville, although it was not printed in *Harper's Magazine* until August, 1856, in an article called "Adventures of Porte Crayon and His Cousins." The "cars," as trains were called then, of the newly established Central Railroad also feature largely in the print. The railroad made the student much more independent than the slower stagecoach, a journey from Lynchburg taking about twenty-four hours before the trains were established.

This view is apparently the first to show the Annex.

72. View of the University from the east, 1853

Robert Mills

73. Robert Mills

Robert Mills (1781–1855) was brought in to design the Annex. As a youth he had worked with Jefferson, who had persuaded him to travel along the eastern seaboard to widen his architectural experience and gave Mills letters of introduction to architects, including one to Bulfinch. Jefferson on June 23, 1808, wrote Mills a letter of recommendation in which are listed "the grounds on which you may justly claim employ." Jefferson's faith was not misplaced, for Mills executed many splendid works, including the monuments to Washington in both Baltimore and Washington.

74. The Annex

The Annex

Although the Annex, or New Hall, was built between 1851 and 1853, this photograph, which appeared in Joseph C. Chandler's 1892 book *Colonial Architecture of Maryland, Virginia, and West Virginia,* is one of the best to have survived. As can be seen the Annex was attached to the north front of the Rotunda and was thrust forward on a great terraced podium with tunneled entrances from ground level. The stone retaining walls remained visible until the late 1950's, when they were covered by the present earth terraces.

A contemporary newspaper account designated this new work as "the splendid additions recently made to the University of Virginia." The opinion of the present University community does not always agree with this accolade, although it was an interesting building with its large public hall and its use of cast iron instead of marble for its Corinthian capitals.

The Annex contained classrooms for drawing, applied mathematics, law, natural philosophy,

75. Iron capital from the Annex

and modern languages. The contractor was a Mr. Hudson, and George Spooner was appointed to "overlook the successive stages of the work." The Public Hall, which occupied the second story of the building and which seated 1,200, was the location of the *first* copy of Raphael's *School of Athens* to come to the University, a copy made by Paul Blaze. News that such a copy was available came through Professor Gessner Harrison in 1850. On December 17, 1850, a committee of alumni— Col. Thomas H. Ellis, John S. Caskie, Socrates Maupin, Benjamin B. Minor, and John R. Thompson— sent a circular to all alumni asking for $2,000. The sum was raised, but it was not until 1854 that an agreement was worked out for purchase. After exhibitions (and great praise) at the Royal Polytechnic Institute, London, the Old Market in Richmond, and the Library Hall in Petersburg, the painting was finally dedicated at the University on April 13, 1857, with an address by Major Preston of Virginia Military Institute.

This copy of the *School of Ath-*

76.   The Public Hall in the Annex

ens was destroyed, together with
the Annex, which had originally
cost about $35,000, by the 1895
fire. The photograph shows the
Public Hall decorated for Founder's Day, 1867, and was donated
to the University's collections by
J. R. Thomson.

77. View of the University of Virginia, Charlottesville, and Monticello, from Lewis Mountain, 1856

78. Detail of exercise ground

View of the University of Virginia, 1856

One of the best views of the mid-nineteenth-century University, this lithograph was "drawn from nature and printed in colors" by F. Sachse and Co. of Baltimore and published by C. Bohn of Washington and Richmond. The rural character of the setting of the University is still quite evident in this bird's-eye view from Lewis Mountain.

The lithograph clearly shows the exercising yard for students, where the exercise master, "roly-poly" M. d'Alphonse, as one student remembered him,

bubbled over with a mixture of buffoonery and wit. . . . At half-past four in the afternoon we assembled

on the grounds and were soon mar-
shalled for our "Preliminary Exercises." . . . They were endless in
variety. I well remember, for example, how gloriously absurd it was to
be one of three hundred men, squat
like toads, hopping along, with tick-
lish gravity, towards some imaginary
pond, to the brisk one, two, tree
[*sic*], four of our vivacious military
Merry Andrew. . . . From these
ever-to-be remembered "Preliminar-
ies" we passed to the parallel bars,
ladders, ropes &c., and finally clus-
tering around our captain, cleared
our throats for supper with some
very enjoyable singing.

One may also see in this view
the road that passed along the
south end of the Lawn, the
crowded and utilitarian character
of the gardens attached to the pavilions, and even the newly established railroad that had freed the
students from a dependence on
horses for transportation to and
from the University. The horse,
however, does figure largely in the
print and even a Conestoga wagon
may be seen.

79. Detail of the railroad and Temperance Hall

80. Conestoga wagon

81. Detail of garden

View of the Lawn, 1856

Bohn's Album and Autographs of the University of Virginia, with a Short History and Beautifully Illustrated with Twenty Steel Engravings and Portraits of the Professors and Officers was issued by Casimir Bohn of Washington and sold by Dr. M. McKennie and G. T. Jones at the University in 1859. It included this view of the Lawn, sometimes known as the "double row of trees print," one of the early engravings to show the Lawn with its trees. In it one is given a quite convincing picture of the terraces, the young trees, and the wall and turnstile at the south end of the Lawn, but the Rotunda is exaggeratedly prominent.

82. View of the Lawn, 1856

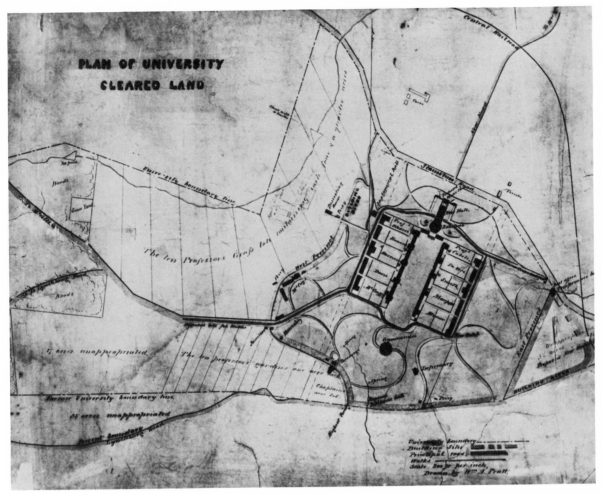

83.   Plan of the University's cleared land, *ca.* 1858

Plan of the University's Cleared Land, *ca.* 1858

William A. Pratt, the University's first superintendent of buildings and grounds, drew this plan showing the University's early expansion. The plan can be dated some time after the building of the gymnasium, which is shown in place, i.e., *ca.* 1858. There are many details of interest on this drawing: the cemetery has been established; the professors have been given a grass lot and a garden allotment; a road surrounds the circumference of the Jeffersonian group of buildings; a *circular* gymnasium and bathhouse has been built; an infirmary (see Illus. 85), a build-

ing that still exists, has been put up; and the Temperance Hall (see Illus. 84) has been erected just outside the east boundary of the University.

In a letter from a student who was at the University between 1855 and 1860 we are told that "D'Alfonce taught gymnastics (1852–61) at an annual charge of $10. About 1858 he erected in the grounds below the infirmary a Russian steam bathing establishment, which was largely patronized by professors and students. We paid $10 a session for a weekly bath."

84. Temperance Hall

Temperance Hall

The temperance movement reached its height at the University between 1842 and 1861. William Wertenbaker, the librarian (see p. 74), is credited with starting the movement among the students, while Professors Minor, McGuffey, and James Cabell supported the movement and worked for total abstinence at the University, although the two Tuckers, who came to be called "wine bibbers," opposed such a move. General John H. Cocke (see p. 39), a noted supporter of temperance, and others gave funds in 1852 for a hall for a group known as the Sons of Temperance, later as the Friends of Temperance, whose members signed a pledge of abstinence. The hall was built in 1855–56, just to the east of the University's property, for about $1,500, and the Sons of Temperance met in the second-floor assembly room. The movement died out after the Civil War, the building reverting to the University. The University Book Store is still in business, but in quarters on the opposite side of the street.

The Infirmary, 1857

In June, 1857, the Board of Visitors appropriated $7,500 for building an infirmary. Professors Cabell and Davis drew up its regulations. For a fee of $5.00 students were entitled, if ill, to prescriptions, lodging, board, a nurse, and a physician, but were allowed the choice of not using these facilities if they paid for private care. The health officer for the University was always a member of the faculty, chosen in rotation.

The building was opened in October, 1858, after an unfortunate typhoid epidemic had swept the grounds. The Infirmary, a rather handsome Victorian building, still survives and houses at present the Air Force R.O.T.C.

85. The Infirmary, 1857

86. McGuffey's ash
87. M for Man

McGuffey's Ash

Among all the trees at the University, the most glorious at present is that called McGuffey's ash. Its enormous size, its splendid shape, and its associations with Professor William H. McGuffey, who lived in Pavilion IX whose garden the tree dominates, have made it one of the pilgrimage points on the grounds.

McGuffey (1800–1873), born in Pennsylvania, became professor of languages, philosophy, and philology at Miami University, Oxford, Ohio, in 1826. After presidencies at various other colleges, he was called to the University of Virginia in 1845 as professor of moral philosophy. Of his *Eclectic Readers,* which so influenced the American mind during the nineteenth century, and of which 122,000,000 copies were sold, the sixth was prepared at the University. The legend is that he used to try his proposed inclusions for the reader at childrens' parties held under the ash. True or not, the legend is charming enough to be perpetuated.

M for Man

This evocative woodcut taken from McGuffey's *Eclectic Spelling-Book* shows a proper Victorian scholar in his study. McGuffey himself might very well have been surrounded by such comfort and such furniture in Pavilion IX.

88. The gatekeeper's lodge

89. Dawson's Row

The Gatekeeper's Lodge

William A. Pratt, the superintendent of buildings and grounds, built this lodge *ca.* 1856, although it is supposed to have been faced with stone and given its Gothic gables at the time the Chapel was built some years later. It was located near the northeast corner of the present Alderman Library, at the intersection of Ivy and McCormick Roads. After Mr. Pratt's tenancy, it was continuously occupied by members of the faculty until its demolition in 1937 to make space for the new library. Because of its Gothic Revival design and the drawbridge over the moat that surrounded it, the lodge was affectionately nicknamed the "Château" or the "Château Front and Back." The photograph was taken about 1920.

Dawson's Row

With money gained by the sale of land devised to the University by Martin Dawson, six buildings were put up in 1859 to house students. A young visitor to some friends quartered in House E during the 1870's described it as "a two-story brick building with four rooms to a floor, and it stood on the road to the cemetery at the 'edge of the wilderness.'" The view reproduced shows Dawson's Row after a sidewalk had been added and each house had been given a portico, *ca.* 1912–13. The Row has given way to the need for space for classroom buildings.

Thomas Jefferson,
by Alexander Galt

In 1854 the Legislature passed a bill commissioning Alexander Galt, of Norfolk and Florence, to create a statue of Thomas Jefferson for the University. It was said that the "poetical genius of Galt" was trusted to make "something . . . beautiful for the rotunda of the University." For his likeness of Jefferson, Galt not only worked from the Gilbert Stuart portrait (see Illus. 6) borrowed from the Randolphs of Edgehill, but he wrote that "Coln. Randolph lent me . . . a suit of [Jefferson's] clothes, boots, coats, socks &c." after Col. Randolph's son had written that "the only other wrapping either my father or aunt remembered, as *often* worn, was a circular Spanish cloak, also with a deep collar, which was embroidered with silver. . . . The square cut coat, and long flapped waistcoat is preserved indeed." After executing a head in clay and plaster, a head which was much liked by the Randolphs, Galt returned to Florence, completed the figure, and had it carved in marble. Although he brought it back to this country late in 1860, it was not delivered to the University until 1861. The outbreak of the Civil War prevented its dedication, an event which did not occur until June, 1868, when the Hon. Hugh Blair Grigsby, a friend and patron of Galt, delivered the address.

At first there had been some discussion of the placement of the statue, with Galt suggesting "the lawn, if I can have a small building erected over it." Professor J. L. Cabell drew a plan suggesting three alternate locations on the

90. Thomas Jefferson, by Alexander Galt

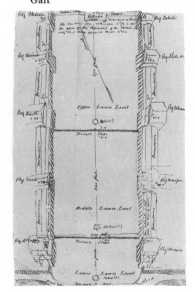

Lawn. The statue has always been in the Rotunda, however, and it still bears the marks of being carried out in a mattress to save it from the 1895 fire.

91. Plan of Lawn, by J. L. Cabell

Student Organizations

Organizations appeared at the University almost as soon as students did. The earliest such group still surviving, the Jefferson Society, was founded July 14, 1825, in No. 7, West Lawn, by students who had broken away from an even earlier group called the Patrick Henry Society, which soon dissolved. The Jefferson Society not only has supported the University's literary magazines but has retained its first aims, "to provide for our common improvement in debate, promote general culture amongst ourselves and those around us, and drill ourselves in all exercises which strengthen for the free duties of citizenship." Among the many famous members of the Jefferson Society have been the Marquis de Lafayette, James Monroe, Edgar Allan Poe, and Woodrow Wilson. Since 1853 the Society has used Jefferson Hall on West Range for its meetings.

The Washington Society, now inactive, was formed as early as November, 1835. It had purposes similar to those of the Jefferson Society, and, after 1869, met in Washington Hall on East Range.

Other student organizations of this pre-Civil War period are listed below with their founding dates. Their symbols, where available, are from an 1892 issue of *Corks and Curls*.

92. Philomathian Society, 1849. Inactive
    Delta Kappa Epsilon, 1852

92.

93.

Parthenon Society, 1852. Inactive *ca.* 1854
93. Phi Kappa Psi, 1853
    Columbian Society, 1854. Inactive *ca.* 1860
94. Phi Kappa Sigma, 1854
95. Beta Theta Pi, 1855
    Theta Delta Chi, 1857
    Phi Gamma Delta, 1858
96. Sigma Alpha Epsilon, 1858
97. Chi Phi, 1859
98. Delta Psi, 1859
    Chi Psi, 1860
99. Sigma Chi, 1860

94.

95.

96.

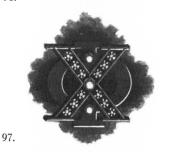
97.

98.

99.

Survival and Consolidation
1865–1917

100. The Lawn, 1868

The Lawn, 1868

This early photograph of the Lawn shows the steps at the base of the dome of the Rotunda still in place. The stone wall and the turnstile at the southern end of the Lawn were used to keep out cattle and other animals. The photograph was a gift to the University of Miss Louise Wills.

101. The University from the east, 1868

The University from the East, 1868

The view of the University from the east emphasizes the rural character of its site during these years. Temperance Hall is on the right, the Annex and its porticoes lengthen the Lawn, and the roofs on East Range have been given their present hip and ridge form, but the parapet on Pavilion X is still in place. The great field is now filled, of course, with the Hospital—School of Medicine complex.

102. The East Gate

The East Entrance to the Grounds

The simple gate that marked the east boundary of the grounds may be seen in this 1893 photograph. It was immediately adjacent to Temperance Hall, whose shadow is seen at the left edge of this print.

In 1912, Mrs. Charles H. Sneff gave the University $20,000 to improve this entrance to the grounds. The new gates were to be a memorial to her husband and a permanent monument to the honor system. They were to be included in a plan to remove the old Temperance Hall. The Sneff Memorial Gates are shown here in a 1922 photograph.

At the time the new gates were put up, a building to house the post office and the bookstore, which had been in Temperance Hall, was erected a little to the east of the site of the old Hall. The new building still survives, but the bookstore has moved across the street.

103. Sneff Memorial Gates

104. Bookstore and tearoom

Anderson Brothers' Store

Although this Victorian monument of commerce has had its store fronts "modernized" many times, its metal-clad upper stories have remained intact. They dominate the Corner and glower at the many generations of students who troop to the area for brief escapes from the academic precincts across the street.

105. Anderson Brothers' Store

Brooks Museum

Completed in 1876, the Brooks Museum was built largely with funds that were donated to the University in 1875 by Lewis Brooks (1793–1877). These funds proved to be not quite enough to finish the museum of natural history and geology. The handsome Victorian building was completed with a gift of $6,000 from Garcy Brooks and the Rev. Samuel Brooks.

Lewis Brooks was born in New Milford, Conn., and was locally educated. Moving to Rochester in 1822, he established himself in the manufacture of woolen cloth to such a degree of success that he retired in 1837, after which he occupied himself with a series of charities.

Although the Brooks Museum was put up in 1875–76, the old photograph of it dates from *ca.* 1900.

106. Brooks Museum

107. Detail of keystone, Brooks Museum

108. Mallet house, 1871

The Mallet House, 1871

Professor John W. Mallet, who came to the University in 1868 and who held the chair of chemistry from 1872, built this house at the end of Dawson's Row where Monroe Hall now stands. It is said to have been put up for about $9,200. Its Victorian Gothicism provided a sharp contrast to the University's earlier classicism. Mr. Mallet favored the admission of women to the University and founded a school of agriculture that later became the Miller School of Biology.

109. Old chemical laboratory

110. A chemistry class in the old laboratory

Chemical Laboratories

The old chemical laboratory was built about 1868–69 and originally had on its entrance front a marble tablet with an inscription from Bacon: "Naturae secreta et artis possibila." Since a collection of technological specimens unsurpassed in the country at that time had been sent to the University by Professor Robert Mallet of London, the laboratory was considered the most complete in the United States. Professor Mallet's son, John (see p. 69), succeeded to the chair of chemistry in 1872.

The building contained a large lecture room, a work room, a store room, and a laboratory. The photograph of the latter shows women in class in accordance with Mr. Mallet's principles.

This building burned in 1917, after which it was rebuilt with a second story and was used first as a biological laboratory, and presently as Peabody Annex. The photograph, *ca.* 1890, shows the back of the laboratory. Note the horse tied to the tree on the right.

After the old chemical labora-

tory burned, a new chemistry
building, designed by Walter D.
Blair of New York, was built near
the hospital. An anonymous donor
gave $5,000 toward this new
building, but J. B. Cobb of New
York donated $60,000 and the
building was named after him. It
was enlarged in 1931 at a cost of
$105,000. The inscription from
Bacon on the old building was repeated on the new.

111.   Cobb Chemical Laboratory

Inscription, Pavilion VII

One of the more personal, though
anonymous, mementos of the
1880's at the University is this inscription laboriously traced with a
diamond on one of the panes of a
window in the second-floor drawing room of Pavilion VII. It reads
"Eclipse of the Moon/June 11,
1881" and takes its place, with the
dignity of recording an event of
some importance, among the other
graffiti.

112.   Inscription, Pavilion VII

113. University Chapel

University Chapel

The Rev. T. D. Witherspoon began raising money for a chapel in 1872, but the University's chaplain, the Rev. Otis A. Glazebrook, carried the project along. The cornerstone was laid in 1885, Professor Schele De Vere delivering the address. Work was slow because of lack of funds, which were partly supplied by both the Young Men's Christian Association and the Ladies Chapel Aid Society, founded in 1883. Mrs. Charles Venable gave $3,000, Mr. Glazebrook gave $1,000 for the organ room, and the Alumni of Kentucky donated the $1,900 organ. Nevertheless, it was the impetus and the devotion of the Ladies Chapel Aid Society that brought the Chapel to completion, and it was they who turned the $30,000 building over to the Board of Visitors in 1890, after Mr. Glazebrook had given the dedication sermon in 1889.

A new organ was given to the Chapel by Mrs. R. O. Price and was dedicated October 11, 1953. It is a memorial to her husband, Robert Osborn Price. The electronic carillon installed in the tower was the gift of the Seven Society.

Truxton Glazebrook and Drs. John A. G. Davis, John Staige Davis, and James L. Cabell are memorialized in windows, while memorial tablets to Drs. Addis Emmet and Gessner Harrison have been fixed on the Chapel's walls.

McCormick Observatory

The history of observatories at the University is a long one, Jefferson having planned one (see Illus. 46) on or near the present site of the McCormick Observatory. Jefferson's building was not built, but another was in 1828 that served until 1859. In 1878 Leander J. McCormick gave a telescope, considered the largest of its kind—32 feet long with an object glass 24¼ inches in clear diameter—made by Alvan Clark and Son of Cambridge, Mass.

The building to house the telescope was given largely by the McCormick family ($18,000), on condition that a chair of astronomy be endowed. A sum of $75,000 was raised, $25,000 from William H. Vanderbilt and $50,000 from other friends and alumni. The first holder of the newly created chair, Ormond Stone, had been nominated by Mr. McCormick in 1882, but the building with its revolving dome resting on steel girders was not finished until 1884.

Leander J. McCormick was born in 1819 (the year of the establishment of the University) in Walnut Grove, Rockbridge County. He held a third interest in his father's reaping machine. Although he joined his brother Cyrus in its manufacture, he retired shortly after 1879.

114. Telescope in McCormick Observatory

Pavilion X, *ca.* 1868–70

Pavilion X retained its parapet until quite late, a feature which gave it a neoclassic air it has lacked since the parapet's removal. The extensive trimming of the trees indicates that they were rapidly reaching the age of replacement at this time. Mrs. Wemple gave the photograph to the University.

115.   Pavilion X, *ca.* 1868–70

Pavilion III, *ca.* 1870

This early photograph of Pavilion III not only shows a group of faculty, including Professors Holmes and Venable, but also the gas lighting system on the Lawn and the parapet of the pavilion, since removed.

116.   Pavilion III, *ca.* 1870

The Rotunda, *ca.* 1870

George Cook of Richmond took this view of the Lawn and the Rotunda in the mid-seventies of the last century. The gentlemen are unidentified, but the custom of using rocking chairs on the Lawn is still in existence. The original clockface in the Rotunda pediment was considerably larger than the present one. Notice also the gas lamps on either side of the steps and the wooden balustrade on the Rotunda's terraces.

Cook also took this photograph of the Library Room on the upper (and now nonexistent) floor of the Rotunda. The room was handsomely scaled with its coupled composite columns—the capitals had been carved by a Mr. Sturtevant—and was used as a repository for University portraits as well as a library. William Wertenbaker, who was appointed librarian on January 30, 1826, by Jefferson, is seen on the left leaning against the guardrail for the statue of Jefferson by Alexander Galt (see Illus. 90). He continued to serve as librarian at intervals until 1879.

That this room was also used for more frivolous purposes may be seen in the drawing by R. H. Laughlin from the *Corks and Curls* of 1894. Although it adapted very well indeed for a ball, it was also used for the more solemn rites of commencements.

117. The Rotunda, *ca.* 1870

118. The Library Room, *ca.* 1870

119.   Thomas Jefferson, by Alexander Galt

120.   A commencement ball in the Rotunda, 1894

The Rotunda, the Annex,
and Brooks Museum, *ca.* 1893

Just before the fire of 1895, the
students who lived on Carr's Hill
saw this aspect of the University
when they walked to class. Note
that the Rotunda has acquired another cupola and that the University is still in an essentially rural
setting. This photograph was included in the Anderson Brothers
Album of 1895.

121. The Rotunda, the Annex, and Brooks Museum from Carr's Hill, 1895

122. Serpentine walls, 1887

The Serpentine Walls

The serpentine walls, though sta-
ble, do not resist a bump. They
have frequently been replaced, in
many cases in locations that were
not original. In the drawing from
Century Magazine of 1887 the
walls look very much out of
plumb. In the photograph of *ca.*
1895 this dilapidation is very apparent and the roughly paved
alley adds to the effect of a neg-
lected area. By 1910 the alleys
had been paved with brick and
the planting had been massed
with picturesque results.

123.   Serpentine walls, *ca.* 1895
124.   Serpentine walls, *ca.* 1910

125. Arcade of West Range, *ca.* 1895

126. Medical Hall

The Arcade of West Range, *ca.* 1895

The walks of the arcades and colonnades were originally paved with brick, some of which survived until the end of the nineteenth century. The stone steps that were added after this photograph was taken are said to have been salvaged from those of the Rotunda after the fire. The walks of the Lawn colonnades, however, had been covered with concrete before this date.

The Medical Hall

Demolished in 1938 in order to make room for the Alderman Library, the Medical Hall, or Anatomical Theater, is the only Jeffersonian building at the University (see Illus. 45) to have disappeared. It had, however, been burned out and subsequently restored in 1886. At its rededication in that year the oration was delivered by Dr. Paul B. Barringer. In the photograph one sees the unpaved West Street before the Medical Hall and the old chemistry laboratory behind it.

Medical Class, 1876–77

Although the University's School
of Medicine suffered from lack of
a hospital, funds, and cadavers –
southern medical students often
preferred northern or British
schools – sizable medical classes
did gather at the University, as
this photograph of the 1876–77
class shows. The tall, bearded
young man in the front row was
Dr. Paul B. Barringer, who re-
dedicated the Medical Building in
1886 and established the University Hospital in 1901. The
photograph itself was taken on
the steps leading to the ground
level of the Annex with the Rotunda in the background. It was
given to the University by Dr. W.
L. Estes, Jr., in 1963.

127.   Medical class, 1876–77

Fayerweather Hall

David B. Fayerweather of New
York gave the $30,000 necessary
to build Fayerweather Hall, which
was designed by Carpenter and
Peebles of Norfolk. At the time it
was built it was supposed to be
one of the best equipped gymna-
siums in the South, and it was certainly a great improvement over
'D'Alfonso's outdoor exercise yard
at the opposite end of the Lawn.
Fayerweather Hall's track was one
of the longest indoor tracks in the
country, and it is said that the
University's first bathtubs were installed in the dressing rooms of
this building.

At the present time the School
of Architecture occupies Fayerweather Hall, but plans to move
into its new building during the
fall of 1969.

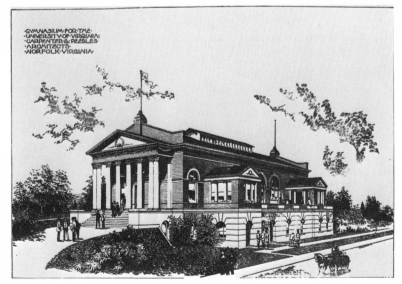

128.   Fayerweather Hall, 1893

129. Interior of Fayerweather Hall, 1895, and Dr. W. A. Lambeth

Lambeth Field

In addition to being the Director of Athletics, Dr. W. A. Lambeth gave twenty-one acres for the construction of Lambeth Field, the first of the University's playing fields with seating for spectators. In 1901 over 48,000 cubic yards of earth were moved in order to create the final grades for the amphitheater and the playing areas. This was an enormous amount of earth to move in prebulldozer days. Lee Taylor was the architect, and it is said the project was finished in 1903 at the unusually low cost of $10,000. The undated photograph reproduced here is much later than the building of the field. (See also p. 159.)

130. Lambeth Field

The Burning of the Annex and the Rotunda

131. The Rotunda fire from the east

The Rotunda Fire

On Sunday morning, October 27, 1895, smoke was seen coming out of the Annex. At once the entire population of Charlottesville rallied to try to save the building and the attached Rotunda, but the fire gained headway. Because the Annex appeared doomed, dynamite was used to try to destroy the portico connecting it to the Rotunda. Two charges of explosives failed, however, and the fire spread into the Rotunda area. Everyone rushed in to save as much as possible, and, more successfully

132. The Rotunda fire from the Lawn

133. The Rotunda fire from the west

than in the Annex (where students had tried to save the copy of the *School of Athens* by ripping it out of its frame only to have fire from behind leap out to burn it), much was saved including the Galt statue of Jefferson.

By five minutes of twelve the roof of the Rotunda was consumed, and soon both the Annex and the Rotunda were in ruins.

134. The Annex after the fire, from the north

The Annex and the Rotunda after the Fire

The extent of the fire's damage was enormous. Not only was the University's principal classroom building completely destroyed, but Jefferson's Rotunda, the dominant feature of his design for the Lawn, was also consumed. Since it had contained the library, the heart of any university, the shock of its destruction was added to the physical losses of the buildings. A sense of this loss is clearly seen in the figures of the spectators in these photographs.

135. The Rotunda after the fire, from the east
136. The Rotunda after the fire, from the west

The Rotunda's Reconstruction

137.   Rotunda during reconstruction, from the north, 1897

Reconstruction of the Rotunda

The fire was not only a turning point in the history of the University – to this day the University community says "before the fire" or "after the fire" in dating University events – but it forced several major decisions that have continuously affected the University ever since. Some of these were, of course, architectural, and one of the first was the decision not to rebuild the Annex.

Stanford White, of the architectural firm of McKim, Mead, and White, was called down from New York to reconstruct the Rotunda, a task he accomplished by giving it a north portico, a feature Jefferson had not included, by combining the first and second floors to make the Library Room one story higher than the original (see Illus. 39), and by building wings on the north front to match the Jeffersonian wings on the south.

Notice the stepping stones, the mud of University Avenue, and the retaining wall of the Annex still in place in Illus. 137. In Illus. 138 the chaos of building is everywhere, but in Illus. 139 the new Rotunda has been virtually completed, although the Corinthian capitals, which were to be carved in place, have not yet been executed.

In the 1902 *Corks and Curls* the students had already taken the new interior to be a subject for

138. North front of the Rotunda, 1897

139. North front of the Rotunda nearing completion, *ca.* 1900

140. McKim, Mead, and White's sectional drawing for the Rotunda reconstruction, 1896

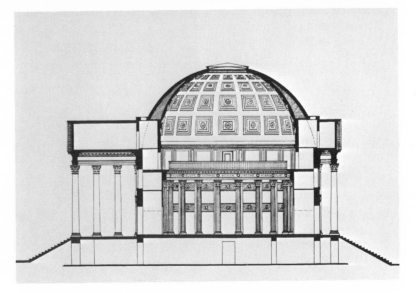

mild satire by printing this verse beneath its photograph:

Lo! The interior of the old Rotunda.
  Within his shrine stands Thomas,
    cold and dumb,
Careless of how the Eli's "make her
    thunder
  With the melodious fife, boys, and
    the drum!"

It should be pointed out that the Jeffersonian Rotunda existed from 1821–22 until 1895, a period of seventy-four years. The "new" Rotunda, started in 1896, will be seventy-three years old in 1969 and is rapidly approaching an antiquity equal to that of the original.

141. New Rotunda interior, 1902

142.   McKim, Mead, and White's drawing for Cabell Hall, *ca.* 1896

Cabell, Rouss, and Cocke Halls

The second major architectural decision forced by the fire was that made to enclose the Lawn at its south end. The delicate task of providing three classroom buildings on this site—Rouss, Cocke, and Cabell Halls—was given McKim, Mead, and White. They designed the three buildings, Rouss and Cocke being similar, using Greek detail rather than Roman, and connected them with a pergola that preserved the view of the mountains.

Cabell Hall, the central one of the three, cut off the nondescript foreground of the southerly view, while its architects took advantage of the sharp descent of the land behind it for concealing the power plant.

Cabell Hall itself was inaugurated during June, 1899. It contained an auditorium for which the firm designed the 1,500 seats of molded plywood, an early use of this new material. The *School of Athens* hanging in Cabell Hall is the *second* copy to be owned by the University. An anonymous gift of an alumnus, it was painted by George W. Breck in Rome, and was presented to the University in April, 1902. The $7,000 Skinner organ was a gift of Andrew Carnegie in 1906 and was dedicated during a recital by Samuel Baldwin on March 18, 1907. The pedimental sculpture above the portico

of Cabell Hall is an allegory based on the quotation "Ye shall know the truth, and the truth shall make you free" from John 8:23. It was executed by George Julian Zolnay, *ca.* 1898.

Rouss Hall, which was built to contain the Department of Physics, now houses the James Wilson Department of Economics and the McIntire School of Commerce. Cocke Hall, which was built primarily as a mechanical laboratory, is now the home of the McIntire Department of Art. Cabell Hall, built as the principal classroom building of the College of Arts and Sciences, still with its annexes serves that purpose.

143. North front of Cabell Hall

144. Cabell Hall from the west, with
      the power plant

Randall Hall

Randall Hall added strength to the University's return to classicism in its building program from the wave of Victorianism and Gothicism that had engulfed it earlier, a return begun with Fayerweather Hall in 1893 and continued with Rouss, Cocke, and Cabell Halls. It was built in 1899 from funds contributed by the estate of W. J. and Belinda Randall of Massachusetts. Its architect was Paul J. Pelz, the designer of the Library of Congress. The photograph reproduced above dates from *ca.* 1915.

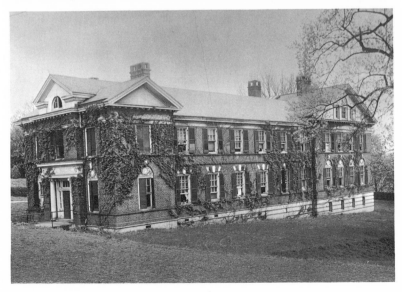

145. Cabell Hall amphitheater, after 1906

146. Cocke Hall

147. Randall Hall

148. University Hospital, *ca.* 1901

The University Hospital

It remained for Dr. Paul B. Barringer to found a hospital for the University. In 1890 he persuaded the faculty to appropriate $150 for planning money. Paul Pelz designed the building. After Lady Nancy Astor gave $600 the foundations were begun. Money accumulated slowly, and when the foundations filled with water they were promptly nicknamed "Paul's Frog Pond." When the Fayerweather Fund gave $9,200 the walls were completed, but the roof was paid for by the University's general funds. The building, containing operating rooms, clinical laboratories, offices, and beds for twenty-five patients, was completed for $25,600.

When Dr. Barringer declared that some day the University would have a hospital with 500 beds, he was considered a visionary, but his prophecy has become a reality. Indeed, plans were drawn up as early as 1904 for additions, the Legislature soon appropriated $31,000, one wing was added in 1906, and a second in 1908.

Madison Hall, *ca.* 1907

John R. Mott, the general secretary of the World's Student Christian Federation, had proposed the need of this building for the Young Men's Christian Association to William E. Dodge, the philanthropist. Before his death, Dodge's widow offered $40,000 if an endowment for the maintenance of the building could be raised. Students, faculty, and friends raised $10,000 in two weeks, and the building was planned by Parish and Schroeder, architects, by April, 1904. Wood-row Wilson dedicated it on October 19, 1905. Madison Hall is now occupied by the School of General Studies.

The photograph dates from *ca.* 1907. Note that although paving has not yet come to Charlottesville, both electricity and the motorcar have arrived.

149. University Hospital, 1909
150. Madison Hall, *ca.* 1907

151.   Civil War Monument, 1906

152.   The Commons

153.   The Commons, now Garrett Hall

Civil War Monument

It was not until 1906 that the Ladies of the Confederate Memorial Association of Albemarle County were able to erect this monument to the 1,100 Confederate dead buried in the University Cemetery. The sculptor was Caspar Buberl, a Bohemian living in New York. His monument is one of the few reminders of the Civil War at the University, which had miraculously survived those difficult years intact.

The Commons, now Garrett Hall

The old Commons was started in March, 1907, and was ready to serve as the University's new dining facility by September, 1908. Designed by McKim, Mead, and White, it was an extraordinarily splendid background for "dieting the students," to use Jefferson's phrase. Waiters, tablecloths, napkins, and even rugs on the floor were maintained until World War II. The Commons was then transformed into a cafeteria, but when the new Student Union opened, the dignified dining hall was turned into the central office of the bursar and renamed Garrett Hall.

Minor Hall

Minor Hall was completed in 1911 for the use of the School of Law, which occupied it until 1932. It was named for John B. Minor, who had been one of the University's preeminent professors of law. The building now houses the Department of Speech and Drama and contains the theater used by the Virginia Players.

154.   Minor Hall

Peabody Hall

Peabody Hall was named for George Peabody, who had set up the Peabody Education Fund. Its trustees gave the University $40,000 for the building, while the University raised another $12,000. Designed by Carlow, Ferguson, and Taylor and built in 1912, Peabody Hall still serves as the home of the University's Curry Memorial School of Education.

155.   Peabody Hall

156. William Wilson Corcoran, by John Adams Elder

William Wilson Corcoran

One of the post-Civil War donors to the University was William Wilson Corcoran (1798–1888). He was born in Georgetown, D.C., the son of an Irish father who became a magistrate, a trustee of Georgetown College, and the postmaster of Georgetown. William Wilson Corcoran was educated privately and at Georgetown College, went into business with his brothers at seventeen, and, after managing real-estate interests of the United States Bank and the Bank of Columbia, opened in 1837 a general banking and brokerage firm. This firm was so successful that during the Mexican War he was able to negotiate a loan of $12,000,000 for the government. Retiring in 1854 he devoted the rest of his life to benefactions, the most notable of which is the Corcoran Gallery in Washington.

His gifts to the University included $1,000 to the chemistry department and $5,000 to the library, given in the 1870's, and endowments in the 1880's for what is now known as the Corcoran Department of History.

The portrait reproduced here was painted in 1877 at White Sulphur Springs by John Adams Elder.

157. Inauguration Day at the University, 1905

Inauguration Day
at the University, 1905

In 1904 the administration of the University was transferred from the chairman of the faculty to a president. Edwin Anderson Alderman was the first of the University's presidents. His inauguration on Founder's Day, 1905, was the occasion for a gathering of many notables, both political and academic, as well as a descendant of Jefferson.

The large statue is one of James Monroe which had originally been at the St. Louis Exposition. The 1905 *Corks and Curls* points out that it was the subject of "outrageous" pranks and prints the following verses about it:

On the Lawn, before this building
    [i.e., Cabell Hall]
Stands a large, imposing statue,
Statue of the dear departed,

Worthy man, respected Statesman,
James Monroe, the great and godly.

This production, vast and awesome,
Came to us from foreign countries,
Even from far-off St. Louis,
From the glorious Exposition.
At the glorious Exposition,
Stood this vast and awesome
Statue. . . .

The "Blind Homer" has taken the place of "this production, vast and awesome." The Monroe statue seems to have disappeared, perhaps destroyed by one of the "outrageous" pranks.

Edwin Anderson Alderman

Edwin Anderson Alderman was born in North Carolina. He had not only helped in the development of the public school system there, but he became the president of its state university. Before he came to the University in 1904 as its first president, he had also served as president of Tulane University.

Eugene Speicher painted this portrait of Dr. Alderman in 1922. It was a gift to the University from the faculty, the alumni, and friends.

158. Edwin Anderson Alderman, by Eugene Speicher

159. "Democracy," a pageant, 1918

"Democracy," a Pageant, 1918

On July 4, 1918, the Rotunda served as the setting for a pageant written by Anna Barringer. Its theme was the triumph of Democracy and Civilization over Autocracy. The photograph shows the climactic moment when Civilization, enthroned, watches the dance of Freedom before banishing Autocracy. The pageant ends with words which are remarkably apropos for our own time:

Make this your pledge
That neither sex, nor creed, nor race,
    nor nation may define
The limits of our service
For the Truth.

160. Woodrow Wilson and fellow members of the Jefferson Society

161. Wilson Memorial Plaque

Woodrow Wilson

Woodrow Wilson (1856–1924), who attended the University's School of Law, graduating in 1881, lived at No. 31, West Range. In the photograph he is shown, the first on the left, with a group of members of the Jefferson Society. After he left the University, he had an academic career at Bryn Mawr, Johns Hopkins, Wesleyan University, and Princeton before he began his life in politics with his governorship of New Jersey, which led, in 1912, to the White House.

He and his presidency are memorialized in the plaque fixed to the wall of the south portico of the Rotunda. It was designed by R. Votolo of New York and was the gift of the classes of 1925 and 1928.

162. The pond

The Pond

The pond, located approximately where the Chapel stands now, was used both as a reservoir for water that was brought to it from another source and was pumped from it to storage tanks in the Rotunda and as an ice pond in the winter, the ice being stored in ice cellars not far away. After the pond was filled, the overgrown ruins of these cellars were promptly dubbed the "petting pits" by the students. The Annex is seen beyond the pond in this photograph of *ca.* 1870–75.

163. Old reservoir

The Old Reservoir

The water supply for the University had preoccupied the University's founders from the first. Jefferson had installed a log pipeline from springs on Observatory Mountain. Tanks had been installed at the top of the Rotunda before the Civil War with steam engines to lift the water from the pond near the present Chapel, the engines being used as late as 1884. In 1869 the reservoir on Observatory Mountain was finished from plans by Major Green Peyton, who later became Proctor. When a

drought was threatened in 1880, this reservoir was enlarged.

The photograph of the reservoir was taken *ca.* 1895. The charming young lady is Miss Estelle Burthe, the stepdaughter of Professor Mallet and the donor of the photograph to the Betts Collection.

164. Skating, *ca.* 1895

Skating, *ca.* 1895

Amusements were few in Charlottesville near the end of the nineteenth century, but on the rare occasions when the ponds froze it was possible to ice skate, a welcome variation on the more usual social contacts. The pond pictured was in the valley between the present library and the tennis courts.

The Golf Links

Beyond Monroe Hill a very rural golf course was established, partially in the area where the Physics Building and the dormitory complex now stand. The urbanization of the University makes it difficult to realize that open country was once so close its precincts.

165.   Golf links

An Engine of the Southern Railroad

The arriving student's first impression of Charlottesville during the 1890's is well summed up in this photograph. It would appear that railroad stations were not much more welcoming then than now.

166.   Engine of the Southern Railroad

Blue Cottage, 1867

Only two years after the Civil War, enough students had returned to the University so that some members of the Jefferson Society occupied this rather ramshackle house called Blue Cottage. The photograph was taken by A. F. Smith in 1867.

167.   Blue Cottage, 1867

168.   Student's room, 1875

A Student's Room, 1875

It is difficult to believe that the
student rooms on the Lawn and
ranges could be so thoroughly
Victorianized as in this example
(Illus. 168). Yet the evidence of
this 1875 photograph of the room
of Dr. Southgate Leigh of Norfolk
is overwhelming. A study of its
detail reveals all the fashionable
accessories necessary to the comfort and amusement of the Victorian student.

169. Carr's Hill, *ca.* 1890

170. Colonnade, 1887

Carr's Hill, *ca.* 1890

It is said that Carr's Hill, first known as Brockenbrough's Hill, was the location of a boarding house for University students as early as 1837. It was owned before the Civil War by a Mrs. Carr who sold it to Judge Alexander Rives. From him it passed into the hands of Mrs. Schele De Vere, from whom the University bought it in 1867 for some $2,000.

The original building was burned *ca.* 1867, but was rebuilt and subsequently improved and enlarged in 1870–71. The dining hall was finished in 1888 and became a part of the University "mess" system, the fee for room, furniture, fuel, lights, food, and servants being $15.00 per month.

The Colonnade, 1887

In spite of such auxiliary students' quarters as Dawson's Row, Blue Cottage, and Carr's Hill, the ideal rooms for the students were on the Lawn. This view from the *Century Magazine* of 1887, looking north from Pavilion VII, demonstrates the triumph of Jefferson's classicism over the Victorian love of clutter, the elegance of his architecture unconsciously affecting both the draftsman and the students.

Football

171. Football team, 1888–89

172. Football, 1895

Not only was the University's academic standing high by the end of the century—it had more doctors in the Army than any other college and more men in Congress (fourteen)—but it was beginning to have a national reputation in sports. An 1894 newspaper article said that "having been placed by foot ball authorities as the next in rank on the gridiron after Princeton, Yale, Harvard and Pennsylvania, Virginia can well claim an equal place with the so-called 'four great colleges of America' in athletics."

The caption, "The Approved Curriculum of the School of Medicine," for the drawing from the 1895 *Corks and Curls,* shows that football could be the subject of a joke as well as a matter of pride.

173. Glee Club, 1894

The Glee Club, 1894

Eli Banana Reunion, *ca.* 1898

The drawing is taken from the Chattanooga *Sunday Times* for February 4, 1894. The *Times* said

the University of Virginia, awakened to the fact by her victories in the scholastic and athletic fields over her grand northern rivals, has decided to show the south that we are not utterly wanting of merit in the musical line, as we have so long been reported to be, by sending out her Glee club, too; and, from the encouraging letters they have gotten from all cities in which they will appear,

they feel that their trip will be a success. . . . The club travels in their special car, and their trip included Richmond, Lexington, Louisville, Nashville, Atlanta and ends at Chattanooga Feb. 6.

By the end of the nineteenth century not only were students' activities very well organized, but it was possible to have reunions of certain student groups. One such reunion was that of Eli Banana, which was founded at the University in 1878. Its membership was based on contributions to the University and on leadership. This photograph of an Eli Banana reunion was a gift to the University from Miss Fanny Hobson.

174. Eli Banana reunion, *ca.* 1898

Student Life

At the turn of the century *Corks and Curls,* the student annual, published a series of drawings of student life. The temptations of a student in 1890 seem very similar to those of today. As for the supper party of 1895, labeled "Academic Department – Parallel Work of the Class in the Science of Society," it would seem that the degree of elegance was a little greater then than now when white ties have almost disappeared.

The dances given in the Rotunda were also elegant, and the young ladies were as frivolous as any we know.

By 1905 the intimidated first-year man looked like this, but he

175. The temptations of a student, 1890

176. A supper party, 1895

TRUE BENEFICENCE.

HE (in the Jefferson Court after the game): Founded the University, you
know.

SHE: Yes, and it was so nice of him, because if he hadn't we would not
have the lovely ball-games.

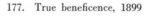

177.   True beneficence, 1899

178.   Cheers, 1901

179. He enters college, 1905   180. The Easter girl arrives, 1905

182.   A student, 1905

183.   When I awake, 1911

181.   He gets his sheepskin, 1905

soon learned to dress grandly for Easters, and he graduated in evening dress, though the custom was changed almost at once by President Alderman, who instituted academic dress. But when he relaxed, the student of 1905 presented a dashing appearance with his wide lapels, his broad-brimmed hat, and his turtleneck sweater.

One of the peculiarities of the University, its outside plumbing for the student rooms on the Lawn and ranges, was caricatured in this 1911 drawing. Since the same conditions are still in existence, the poor chilled student may still be seen on the Lawn.

Student Organizations

Of those secret societies formed between the Civil War and World War I, the most secret and perhaps the most interesting is the Seven Society. Even the date of its founding is unknown, but its gifts to the University have been numerous, for it has set up loan funds and scholarships, made gifts to needy students, and given the University its carillon and its mace. None of the members are known until their deaths, when the University's carillon is tolled in a special seven-tone sequence at the hours of their burials.

The founding dates of the post-Civil War organizations are given below with their symbols, taken in part from a *Corks and Curls* of 1892, except for that of the Seven Society.

184. Alpha Tau Omega, 1868
185. Pi Kappa Alpha, 1868
186. Zeta Psi, 1868
187. Kappa Sigma, 1869
      Sigma Nu, 1870
188. Kappa Alpha, 1873

185.

186.

188.

184.

187.

189.

189. Phi Delta Theta, 1873
    Eli Banana, 1878
    The German Club, 1888.
        Dance Society
    13 Society, 1889
    T.I.L.K.A., 1889
    Phi Delta Phi, 1890. Law
    PK Society, 1895. Dance So-
        ciety
    Z Society, late 19th century
    IMP, (?)
190. Seven Society, *ca.* 1900 (?)
    Raven Society, 1904
    Delta Phi, 1907
    Phi Sigma Kappa, 1907
    Sigma Phi Epsilon, 1907
    Phi Beta Kappa, 1908
    Phi Alpha Delta, 1910. Law
    Theta Chi, 1914
    Phi Epsilon Pi, 1915
    Zeta Beta Tau, 1915

190.

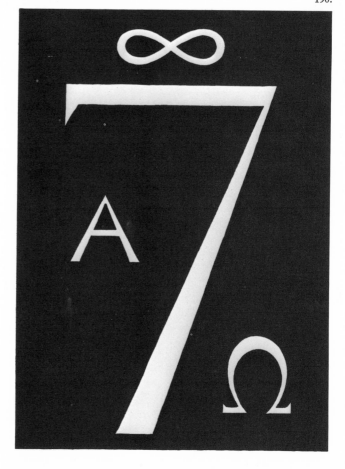

Expansion
1918–the Present

191.   The Lawn from the air, 1961

The Lawn from the Air, 1961

Aerial photography has allowed Jefferson's beautiful plan to be seen as a whole for the first time. One may see not only the Lawn, Rotunda, and ranges in this photograph, taken before the restoration of the east gardens, but many of the additions to Jefferson's original design may be picked out. At the lower right Rouss, Cocke, and Cabell Halls close the south end of the Lawn. The Hospital complex is in the upper righthand corner. The Chapel and Brooks Museum may be seen on either side of the Rotunda, while Madison Hall is opposite it. At the bottom are Monroe, Garrett, and Minor Halls and the McIntire Amphitheater, while tucked away to the right of Rouss Hall is the original Infirmary. The photograph is a gift to the University of the Commission for the 200th Anniversary of the Founding of Charlottesville.

The Lawn

192. The Lawn

The Lawn

Even with modern photography, it is very difficult to give a comprehensive view of the Lawn from the ground, although this romantic print captures many of its aspects.

193. The Rotunda

194. Pavilion I, West Lawn

The Rotunda

The Rotunda was "restored" a second time in 1938–39. With the financial help of the Public Works Administration, the concrete balustrades and the concrete steps that had been installed after the 1895 fire were removed, and the present marble steps and balustrades were put in place. The work moved swiftly, beginning on September 26, 1938, and ending on June 1, 1939.

The Pavilions

The pavilions have suffered many changes since they were first designed by Jefferson. There is only one that has not been enlarged, Pavilion III. None house classes anymore, although Pavilion III, the "Graduate Pavilion," and Pavilion VI, the "Romance Pavilion," continued to do so for some time after World War II. Pavilion VII, the Colonnade Club, has been enlarged more than the others in order to provide accommodations for unmarried faculty. All the roof parapets are gone (cf. the drawings for Pavilions III, V, VIII, IX, and X [Illus. 15, 16, 17, 20, 26]), as are the original Chippendale railings except those on the balconies under the porticoes. It should also be noted that the ridge roofs above the students' rooms have been put on over the flat roofs Jefferson had installed.

195. Pavilion III, West Lawn

196. Pavilion V, West Lawn

197. Pavilion VII, West Lawn

198. Pavilion VII, West Façade

199. Pavilion IX, West Lawn

201.   Pavilion IV, East Lawn
202.   Pavilion VI, East Lawn

200.   Pavilion II, East Lawn

203.   Pavilion VIII, East Lawn
204.   Pavilion X, East Lawn

The Colonnades

The colonnades, and the arcades, were conceived functionally as well as aesthetically. Their shade and their shelter are very welcome during hot or inclement weather. The students have given the colonnades another use, and that is as a storage place for their firewood.

205.   Firewood and students

206.   The colonnades

Cabell Hall

Although the closing of the south end of the Lawn has been disliked almost continuously since the construction of Cabell Hall, it is possible, under certain conditions, for the Hall and the Lawn to coalesce into a romantic view.

207. Cabell Hall

East Range

The original hotels on East Range have almost disappeared under their various alterations and extensions, but the arcades, in spite of the hipped roofs that have been added, still retain much of their early aspect.

208. East Range

One West Range

One West Range, originally one of the hotels (see Illus. 34), or boarding houses, has had many uses during its existence, including its occupation by the Medical School at one point. Finally it became the headquarters of the *Virginia Quarterly Review* in 1929, and was recently restored to its Jeffersonian plan.

209. One West Range

The Gardens

West Lawn Gardens

In 1948 the Garden Club of Virginia began allocating the proceeds from its Historic Garden Week to the gardens of the pavilions on West Lawn at the University. The walls were restored to their original positions, and the gardens were designed by Alden Hopkins. The presentation of the five gardens on the west was made in Cabell Hall on April 24, 1952. In the aerial view the completed gardens may be seen on the right. Those on the left (east) have not yet been changed from the design instituted by Dr. Lambeth during the early part of this century.

210. Serpentine walls under construction, Pavilion V

211. Aerial view of the University from the north

212. Newly planted garden at Pavilion I

213. Aerial view of the East Lawn gardens, *ca.* 1920

214. The cross drive, East Lawn gardens, before 1940

East Lawn Gardens

Beginning in 1960, the Garden Club of Virginia again devoted the proceeds of Historic Garden Week to the University gardens, this time those for the pavilions on East Lawn. With a considerably steeper slope than those on the west, and with only small portions of the original walls still in place, the gardens on East Lawn presented much greater problems than those that had been faced during the restorations on the west. The transformation may clearly be seen by comparing the two aerial photographs.

The gardens for East Lawn were dedicated on May 4, 1965, by an address entitled "Restoration in Virginia" delivered by Governor Albertis S. Harrison, Jr. The Garden Club of Virginia affixed a bronze plaque to the garden wall of Pavilion II with the following inscription:

215. Aerial view of the East Lawn gardens, 1965

THESE GARDEN WALLS
originally designed and built by
Thomas Jefferson, 1821–1824, as a part of his architectural plan for
the University of Virginia were restored and the enclosed gardens
planted as a gift of
The Garden Club of Virginia, 1965.
The gardens are a creation of three Landscape Architects.
The basic plan by Alden Hopkins
and design and execution by Donald Howard Parker
and Ralph Esty Griswold, Consultant.

216. Foundations, serpentine walls, Pavilion X

217. Restoration of serpentine walls, Pavilion X

218. Garden, Pavilion VIII

219. The long walk after restoration of the East Lawn gardens

220. Monroe Hall, south front

221. Memorial fountain, Monroe Hall, north front

Monroe Hall

Monroe Hall, finished in 1929 but not occupied until January 1930, was designed by Walter D. Blair of New York, John K. Peebles of Norfolk, R. E. Lee Taylor of Baltimore, and Edmund S. Campbell of the School of Architecture. Its cost was some $260,000, and it is presently the headquarters for the Graduate School of Business Administration, which was authorized in 1952, the first in the South.

The exedra before the north front of Monroe Hall is a memorial to the Hon. Frank Hume (1843–1906). It is inscribed as follows: "A devoted Virginian who served his native state in civil war and legislative hall."

222. Clark Memorial Hall

223. The central hall, Clark Memorial Hall

224. Judge Advocate General's School, 1968

Clark Memorial Hall

William Andrews Clark, who had studied law under Dean William Minor Lile at the University with the class of 1899, provided the funds to build Clark Memorial Hall for the School of Law. The building, dedicated in 1932, was given in memory of Mr. Clark's wife, Mabel Foster Clark. The great central hall was built primarily of Roman travertine and marble and contains two murals by Allyn Cox, allegories on Mosaic and Roman law.

The library in Clark Memorial Hall is the largest law library in the South.

The Judge Advocate General's School of the United States Army occupies a building located directly to the rear of Clark Memorial Hall and in addition utilizes part of the Hall in providing instruction in military law.

Bayly Building,
University of Virginia
Museum of Fine Arts

Mrs. Evelyn May Bayly Tiffany's bequest of $100,000 in memory of her parents and a grant of $38,000 from the Public Works Administration enabled the University to build, in 1934–35, the Bayly Building to house the University of Virginia Museum of Fine Arts. It was designed by Edmund S. Campbell.

The University's collections were housed there, and the formal portrait of Jefferson painted by Bass Otis from the life portrait (see Illus. 7) may be seen in the photograph of the galleries. The urn-shaped knife boxes seen on the right of the same photograph were included in Mrs. Tiffany's bequest, for she gave the University the contents of her dining room, including the portraits of her family. Although the Museum has been inoperative for a decade, it is hoped that the establishment of the new Fine Arts Center will allow the Bayly Building to be returned to its original purpose.

225. Bayly Building, University of Virginia Museum of Fine Arts

226. Upper galleries, University Museum of Fine Arts

Thornton Hall

Thornton Hall, built in 1936 from a Public Works Administration grant of $316,495 and the sale of bonds, has had many additions since that time as the School of Engineering has grown. The building was named as a memorial to William Mynn Thornton who was Chairman of the Faculty, 1888–96; Dean of Engineering, 1904–25; and Professor Emeritus of Applied Mathematics until his death in 1935.

Alumni Hall

The Alumni Association is one of the oldest organizations at the University, having been formed in 1838. It occupied its present headquarters in 1936, but the building was remodeled and very much expanded in 1950 as the Alumni Association's war memorial. The architects for this $150,000 enlargement were Edmund S. Campbell, W. E. Stainback ('28), and Louis Scribner ('29). The garden walls were given anonymously in 1955.

There are now over 40,000 living alumni, of whom some 10,000 are active members of the Alumni Association. Their dues support the Association's activities, including the *Alumni News* which is issued six times a year.

227.   Thornton Hall
228.   Alumni Hall

229. Construction of Alderman Memorial Library, 1937

Alderman Memorial Library

The decision to build a new library broke two Jeffersonian traditions, for it moved the library away from the Rotunda and it meant the destruction of the Jeffersonian Anatomical Theater. Such a decision was necessary, however, if the University's collections were to be housed in such a way that they could be used by the faculty and students, the space in the Rotunda having proved woefully inadequate for reading, research, and storage.

President Alderman began the search for funds for a new library building in 1924, but it was not

230. Alderman Memorial Library, 1965

until the establishment of the Public Works Administration that President Newcomb was able to secure a grant of $427,909, with which he began the building.

The relation of Alderman Memorial Library to the old Anatomical Theater, and to West Range, may be seen in the construction photograph of 1937. The new building, designed by Taylor and Fischer, was officially opened at 8:30 A.M., May 11, 1938, when President Newcomb withdrew the first book, one concerning President Alderman's orations.

The University's library is the third largest in the South, but its manuscript collection is unequaled. Among the more than five million manuscripts are the document of Cornwallis' surrender at Yorktown, the manuscript of Walt Whitman's *Leaves of Grass*, Tennessee Williams' *Glass Menagerie*, and papers of Jefferson, Poe, Stephen Crane, Carter Glass, and the Randolph, Cocke, and Bruce families.

The library has also attracted many specialized collections. Some 12,000 items were donated in 1938 to form the Tracy W. McGregor Library of American history, English literature, and southeastern American literature. The McGregor Room was installed to care for this collection, which is a growing one thanks to the continuing interest of the McGregor Trustees.

The Garnett Room houses the Muscoe Garnett Home Library,

231. Browsing Room, Alderman Memorial Library

232. McGregor Room, Alderman Memorial Library

233. Garnett Room, Alderman Memorial Library

234. Barrett Room, Alderman Memorial Library

235. Addition to Alderman Memorial Library

while other collections that have come into the library are the Edward L. Stone Collection on the history of printing; the Sadlier-Black Collection of the Gothic novel; the Miles Poindexter Collection; the Charles Darwin Collection, one of the greatest in the world; the Cotton Mather Collection; and the continually increasing William Faulkner Collection, which is the largest concentration of Faulkner material in the world, generously given to the University by Linton R. Massey.

The Barrett Collection, the gift of Clifton Waller Barrett, is the most important gathering of American literature in existence. At the time it was sent to the University from New York, where Mr. Barrett had been assembling it since 1940, it was said to be the most valuable shipment of literary material ever received by a university in this country. It, too, is a continuing collection, and many gifts have been added to it since its dedication on April 30, 1960.

Just as Presidents Alderman and Newcomb had difficulty finding the funds to build Alderman Memorial Library, so have their successors encountered the same difficulty in finding funds for its desperately needed additions. The first such addition, costing $1,423,495, was designed by J. Russell Bailey, and went into service, primarily as stack space for 750,000 books, in 1967.

Blandy Farm

In 1927 Graham F. Blandy gave the University a farm in Clarke County, near Winchester. It consisted of 65 acres of orchards, 50 acres of woods, 130 acres of experimental plots, and 500 acres of cultivated and grazing land. The University now uses it as the center of the Miller School of Biology and Agriculture, a school which was established by the bequest of Samuel Miller in 1869. The photo- graph, of *ca.* 1957–58, shows the buildings of the farm, which in 1940 were converted into laboratories, a dormitory, and a library.

236. Blandy Farm

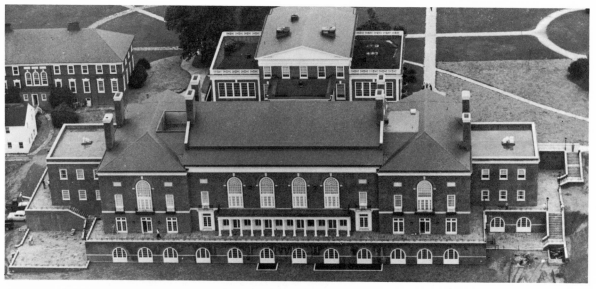

237. Newcomb Hall

238. Lounge, Newcomb Hall

239. Flaxman relief, Newcomb Hall

Newcomb Hall

Newcomb Hall, the student union, was completed in 1958. It had been designed by Eggers and Higgins to contain two cafeterias, a grill, bowling alleys, darkroom facilities, lecture rooms, lounges, and a ballroom. Its bookstore now contains the largest stock of softbound books in Virginia.

In the northern lobby is a plaster relief by John Flaxman given by the University College of London after World War II. It was retrieved from the Flaxman Gallery there, a gallery which had been bombed, and it was given as a symbol of the intellectual kinship that had linked the two institutions when they were first established (see pp. 45 and 46).

The building is named in honor of John Lloyd Newcomb, the University's second president.

240. Aerial view of the Medical Complex

241. Dedication of the new Hospital

The Medical Complex

The medical complex at the University is in an almost constant process of enlargement; at the time of writing a very large medical education building is being added.

The new hospital, which momentarily relieved crowding, was dedicated on April 14, 1961, with both former President Colgate W. Darden, Jr. (at the podium), and President Edgar F. Shannon, Jr., present for the ceremonies. The glimpse of the kitchen in the old hospital shows how rapidly once "modern" facilities change.

The Medical School Building was constructed between 1927 and 1929 and was dedicated on October 22, 1929, by Dr. Roy Lyman Wilbur, Secretary of the Interior. Its cost, $1,400,000, was defrayed by $800,000 from the General Education Board of Virginia, $250,000 from the state's treasury, and contributions from the Alumni Board of Trustees, the Oliver Hazard Fund, Thomas Fortune Ryan, Charles Steele, John Barton Payne, Thomas Jefferson

242. Kitchen in the old Hospital

243. Medical School

Coolidge, John Thomas Lupton, Carter Lupton, William Events Benjamin, Frederick William Scott, Joseph Manuel Hartfield, John Lee Pratt, Hugh Hampton Young, Henry Morgenthau, Louis Baum, and Mary Branch Munford.

McKim Hall, built to house the nurses, cost over $190,000 in 1930–31. These funds were partially donated by Randolph Harrison McKim ($68,698.09), the balance being funded by the Legislature. Nurses training began in 1901, but the present School of Nursing was established in 1928 with $50,000 given by the Graduate Nurses Association of Virginia.

244. McKim Hall

245. Laboratory in the Medical School

246. Aerial view of Gilmer Hall, 1962

Gilmer Hall

Named for Francis Walker Gilmer (see p. 43), who helped to assemble the original faculty, Gilmer Hall takes its place in the University's new Science Center, housing the life sciences. It was completed in 1963 at a cost of $3,000,000, its equipment including a $40,000 microscope. Its superb amphitheater, fitted with every kind of electric and electronic device, is often shared with the University community. Here President Shannon is acting as chairman for a lecture by Dumas Malone, the University's Biographer in Residence.

247. Entrance to Gilmer Hall, 1963

248. Interior of Gilmer Hall amphitheater, 1963

249. **Atomic Reactor Building**

Atomic Reactor

The atomic reactor was the first of the nuclear facilities to be established at the University. Although all possible safety measures were taken in its construction, its isolated site on Observatory Mountain serves as a further precaution in the protection of the University and Charlottesville.

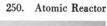

250. **Atomic Reactor**

Nuclear Physics Laboratory

The Nuclear Physics Laboratory, designed by Rawlings and Wilson, was completed in 1965. It was the second building to be associated with nuclear technology to be put up on Observatory Mountain. The $1,200,000 structure houses a 52-foot tower with a 5,500,000-watt Van de Graaff accelerator, and there is, in addition, a 75,000,000-volt electron accelerator.

251. Nuclear Physics Laboratory

252. Accelerator in Nuclear Physics I Laboratory

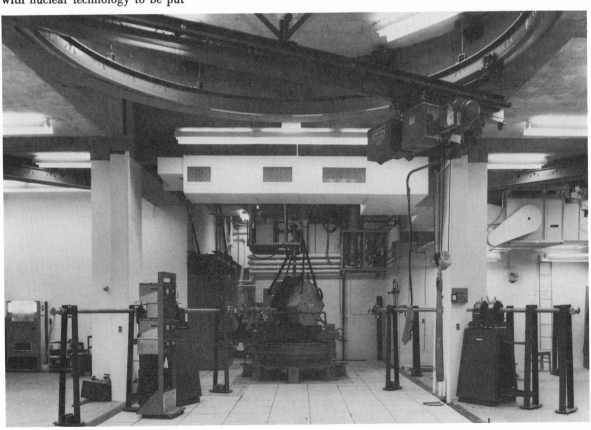

253. Observatory at Fan Mountain

254. Interior of Observatory with reflector telescope

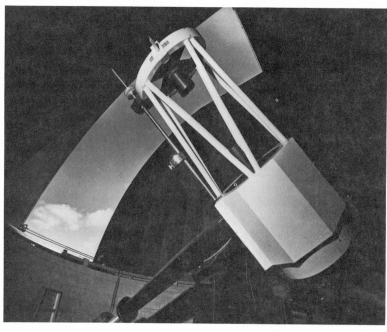

Observatory at Fan Mountain

Nineteen miles south of Charlottesville, the University's newest observatory at Fan Mountain is shared with the National Radio Astronomy Observatory. The University's astronomy faculty and the staff of the National Radio Astronomy Observatory make up one of the largest bodies of astronomers in the world. The 32-inch reflector telescope at Fan Mountain may be fitted with a photometer and a spectrograph. In a smaller dome it is possible to classify stars according to temperature through the use of the 10-inch astrograph. In addition to the two domes there is a three-story building for housing the staff during protracted periods of observation.

New Chemistry Building

The new chemistry building, completed in 1968, was designed by Stainback and Scribner with Anderson, Beckwith, and Haible of Boston as consultants. It relieves the badly crowded conditions of old Cobb Laboratory (see Illus. 111) and is the newest addition to the University's growing Science Center. Ervin R. Van Artsdalen has said that this $5,000,000 building provides the best collegiate laboratories in the country.

255. New Chemistry Building

256. Academic procession for the Centennial, 1921

McIntire Amphitheater

The Centennial of the University, which should have been celebrated in 1919, was not properly marked until 1921 because World War I had delayed the plans for it. The academic procession that year for the first time marched into the new McIntire Amphitheater, the gift of Paul Goodloe McIntire, on June 2. The amphitheater, though planned as early as 1911 by Warren H. Manning of Boston, was not completed until 1921 and was first used for the Centennial exer-

cises. The speakers on this occasion were Sir Auckland Geddes, the British Ambassador, the Hon. John Bassett Moore, of the Class of 1880, and Hamilton Fish, professor of international law and diplomacy at Columbia University.

257. McIntire Amphitheater

258. Centennial speakers in McIntire Amphitheater, 1921

259.   Pilgrimage to Monticello, 1924

Pilgrimage to Monticello, 1924

The Thomas Jefferson Memorial Foundation was formed in 1923 for the purpose of purchasing and preserving Thomas Jefferson's home, Monticello. It was so purchased for $500,000. Money was solicited from the entire country and even from the nation's school-children, who were asked for their nickels. On the University's Founder's Day of 1924—i.e., Jefferson's birthday, April 13—a great procession of thousands of donors for the purchase of Monticello, children and adults, formed on the Lawn for a pilgrimage to

264. The University Mace   265. The mace in use, academic procession, 1965

The University Mace

The Seven Society presented a mace, an ensign of authority to be carried before an official in a procession, to the University on April 13, 1961. The photograph of the academic procession shows how the mace is carried. One of the symbols that the mace displays is a relief of the seated statue of Jefferson, now located at the south end of the Lawn. The original statue is by Karl Bitter, who executed it for the Louisiana Purchase Exhibition at St. Louis in 1904. It had been given the University by Charles R. Crane at the sculptor's request, but was not unveiled until Founder's Day of 1915.

266. John Lloyd Newcomb and Mrs. Franklin D. Roosevelt

John Lloyd Newcomb and Mrs. Franklin D. Roosevelt

After President Alderman's sudden death on April 29, 1931 – he was stricken with apoplexy while traveling to a speaking engagement and died in Connellsville, Pa., where he had been taken off the train – John Lloyd Newcomb, then the dean of the Department of Engineering, was appointed acting president, and subsequently president. One of his early official duties was to welcome Mrs. Franklin D. Roosevelt, who visited the University soon after his appointment.

267. President and Mrs. Colgate W. Darden, Jr.

President and Mrs. Colgate W. Darden, Jr.

The third president of the University was Colgate W. Darden, Jr., who succeeded John Lloyd Newcomb in 1947. Mr. Darden, who was born in Southampton County, studied at the University from 1914 until 1916, when he joined the Lafayette Escadrille, suffering serious injuries in a plane crash just before the end of World War I. He returned to the University, graduating in 1922, studied law at Columbia in 1923, and received a Carnegie Fellowship in International Law in 1924 for study at Oxford. After establishing himself in law practice in Norfolk, he entered the House of Delegates, served three terms in the House of Representatives, and was elected Governor of Virginia in 1941.

Carr's Hill, the presidential house at the University, seen here behind the Dardens, was started in 1907 after designs by McKim, Mead, and White. Not finished until 1909, its original cost was about $28,000.

Colgate W. Darden, Jr., and Edgar F. Shannon, Jr.

At the time of the transfer of the presidency from Colgate W. Darden, Jr., to Edgar F. Shannon, Jr., in 1959, this photograph recorded a conference between the two in Mr. Darden's office in Pavilion VIII, East Lawn.

268. Colgate W. Darden, Jr., and Edgar F. Shannon, Jr.

President and Mrs. Edgar F. Shannon, Jr., 1959

The University's fourth president is Edgar F. Shannon, Jr., elected in 1959. A native of Virginia, he knew the University well as a child, for his father, a professor at Washington and Lee, spent many summers teaching here. Mr. Shannon received the Algernon Sydney Sullivan Award as the most outstanding graduate at Washington and Lee in 1939. Receiving an M.A. from Duke University in 1941, he entered the Navy. Narrowly escaping death when his ship, the U.S.S. *Quincy,* was sunk with a loss of 370 dead and 167 wounded, he went on to see action in nine campaigns in the Pacific. After World War II, he took up graduate work at Harvard, gaining an M.A. with his work on Alfred Lord Tennyson. As a Rhodes Scholar he received his Ph.D. from Merton College, Oxford. Although he returned to Cambridge to join the Harvard faculty, he was in England again during 1953–54 as a holder of both a Fulbright and a Guggenheim Fellowship. His many articles and books are a partial harvest from these years of study. But his wise guidance of the University through this decade of its most rapid development, intellectually and physically, has also been a splendid harvest for the institution.

269.   President and Mrs. Edgar F. Shannon, Jr., 1959

President and Mrs. Calvin Coolidge

On Thanksgiving Day, 1928, President and Mrs. Coolidge were guests of the University for the Virginia – North Carolina football game. Some 20,000 spectators had gathered for the game, which was won 24–20 by North Carolina. President and Mrs. Coolidge spent the weekend at Swannanoa, the great marble house at the top of the Blue Ridge, and on Sunday attended services at the church in Staunton where Woodrow Wilson's father had been pastor.

270.   President and Mrs. Calvin Coolidge

Franklin Delano Roosevelt, 1940

When President Roosevelt addressed the University community on June 10, 1940, he gave what has since come to be known as his "stab-in-the-back" speech. It was called that because, referring to his efforts to keep Italy out of World War II, he said, "The hand that held the dagger has struck it into the back of its neighbor." Over 2,000 people were assembled for his speech, and his visit to the University was celebrated by the world premiere of the *Testament of Freedom*, composed for the occasion by Randall Thompson, then the music director at the University.

271.   Franklin Delano Roosevelt, 1940

272.   President Harry S Truman, 1948

President Harry S Truman, 1948

President Harry S Truman came
to Charlottesville to speak at the
ceremonies at Monticello on July
4, 1948. During the course of this
visit, he used the Colonnade Club
(Pavilion VII) as his headquarters. He is here seen driving out
from the Club with the West
Range and guards, photographers,
and spectators in the background.

273. Dinner for President Sukarno, 1956

Dinner in the Rotunda

The "new" Rotunda has frequently been used for banquets since its restoration after the 1895 fire. The Jefferson Society has dined there, the Virginia Chapter of the American Institute of Architects celebrated the centenary of its organization there, and it has been the scene for banquets honoring Robert Frost, other distinguished visitors, and retiring faculty members, thus continuing the tradition begun when Lafayette was entertained in the unfinished "first" Rotunda in 1824 (see p. 34). The photograph reproduced here is of the banquet given by President Darden for President Sukarno of Indonesia during his world tour in the spring of 1956. The Indonesian Foreign Minister, Abul Gani, and Mrs. Darden may also be seen at the table. The Indonesian party was accompanied by the United States Ambassador to Indonesia, Hugh S. Cumming, Jr., who had been a member of the University's Class of 1924.

274.   Senator John F. Kennedy

John F. Kennedy

presidency, during his
Senate, John F. Ken-
the University to be
speaker at a Legal
held in the Memo-
um on March 10,
rty included his fa-
Jacqueline, and his
rt, who was chair-
al Forum in 1951,
ho in 1958 was a
aw student at the
t had been arranged
to visit the University
his election as President, but
is tragic death occurred before
the date that had been suggested.

Before
term in the
nedy came
the principa
Forum din
1958. His pa
ther, his wife,
brothers, Rob
man of the Leg
and Edward, w
second-year
University.
for him
after
h

Mrs. Lyndon Baines Johnson and
Mrs. Hubert H. Humphrey

During a tour in connection with
the President's Visit America First
campaign, Mrs. Lyndon Baines
Johnson, accompanied by Mrs.
Hubert Humphrey, visited the
University on May 11, 1965. She
was especially interested in the
garden restorations and spent
some hours examining the gardens
as well as the Jeffersonian buildings.

275. Mrs. Lyndon Baines Johnson and
      Mrs. Hubert H. Humphrey

276. Mad Bowl, 1965

Mad Bowl

Mad Bowl (behind Madison Hall)
seems to have been used for athletics from the time Fayerweather
Hall was the gymnasium for the
University. It is now used both
formally and informally, though
its formal use is presently confined
to some intramural events. Only
the imagination of
will limit the sports t
there during a session of th
versity.

Lacrosse at Lambeth Field

After World War II lacrosse had a
revival at the University, and during the 1950's the student body
produced some nationally rated
players. The photograph shows a
game between the University and
a joint team made up of men from
Oxford and Cambridge on an
American tour. It was held at
Lambeth Field, which remained
the University's field for sports
other than football after Scott
Stadium (see Illus. 281 and 282)
was built.

277. Lacrosse at Lambeth Field

Memorial Gymnasium, before 1950

The Memorial Gymnasium was put up in 1922–24 in memory of the 2,700 students and alumni who had served the nation in World War I. At that time it was the third largest gymnasium in the East. Although there was no formal dedication, it was opened with a basketball game played with Randolph Macon, a game which was won handily by the University, 41–14. The money for the gymnasium came from three sources. The State granted $50,000; President Alderman raised $100,000; and the students contributed $150,000.

The reflecting pool, which was used for skating in the winter, was drained and filled in 1952. It had become fouled with mud which caused trouble with the drainage system at the gymnasium.

278. Memorial Gymnasium, before 1950
279. Boxing Conference Tournament, 1935

Boxing

Between the two wars, boxing was one of the great sports at the University. In 1935 when the Conference Tournament was held in Memorial Gymnasium the event was able to draw an enormous crowd. The co-captains of the 1938 team were Louis Schmidt of Avon, N.J., the national lightweight champion (on the right in the photograph) and Maynard Harlow, a welterweight, of Ivy, Va. The man in the center was the remarkable boxing coach Johnny La Rowe. His teams had been highly successful, although he had reached the advanced age of 79 by the time this picture was taken.

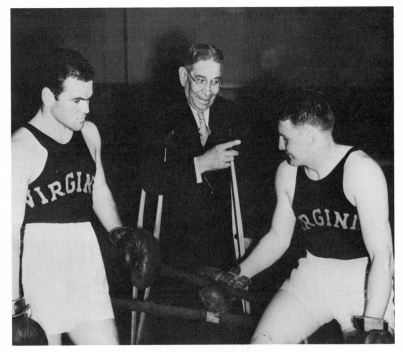

280.   Maynard Harlow, Coach Johnny La Rowe, and Louis Schmidt, 1938

Scott Stadium

Frederick W. Scott, former Rector of the University, gave over $300,000 to the fund for building Scott Stadium. It was dedicated on October 15, 1931. Following the ceremonies in which both former Governor Harry F. Byrd and Lieutenant Governor James H. Price took part, there was a football game between the University and the Virginia Military Institute. It must be recorded, reluctantly, that V.M.I. won by a score of 18 to 3.

281.   Scott Stadium

282. Aerial view, Scott Stadium

University Hall

University Hall was built to provide the University with a field
house and an auditorium capable
of seating its increasing student
body. The Alumni Association,
and later the Alumni Fund, raised
about $500,000 of its cost in a
drive dubbed "Operation Leadership," begun in 1959; the Legislature appropriated $2,367,692; and
the remainder of its $4,000,000
cost was obtained from revenue
bonds and student fees. Designed
by Baskerville and Son of Rich-

283. University Hall

mond with Anderson, Beckwith, and Haible of Boston as consultants, the auditorium seats 9,486, but for basketball games it will hold 8,466. Since it may be converted into an auditorium for theatrical and musical events, 2,969 upholstered seats were installed. Care was taken to provide an acoustical shell for these occasions that assures the proper acoustics for the smaller audiences.

The dome and indeed the building, which was completed in 1965, are of such a size as have not been seen at the University before, but, instead of upsetting the University's scale, it has provided a new focus in the landscape. The prestressed concrete dome contains more than 106 miles of cable.

284. Interior, University Hall

285. Interior of University Hall arranged for a stage presentation

Seal, a University Mascot

Of all the various mascots that the University has acquired, Seal was undoubtedly the most popular. His cross-eyes gave him an appeal his complacency might not have gained for him. He attended almost every University function, athletic or not, for some thirteen years, and his presence on the platform with orators or musicians was almost *de rigueur*. But his most endearing act occurred when he publicly showed the utmost contempt for the University's opponent at a trying and difficult football game. When he died on December 9, 1954, his funeral procession was led by the University band, a Cadillac filled with student dignitaries, and a hearse. A throng of about 2,000 attended his burial just outside the walls of the University Cemetery at which a eulogy was delivered by Dr. Charles L. Fankel, the physician for the football team. Nasty, Seal's heir apparent, wore a black mourning band on his paw for the occasion.

286. Seal, a University mascot

287. William Dudley, *ca.* 1940

William Dudley

William Dudley, born in Bluefield, W.Va., became one of the University's outstanding football players. Named an All-American quarterback when he was an 18-year-old junior, his most spectacular feat that year was an 87-yard touchdown runback of Tennessee's kickoff. He was called the "Bluefield Bullet" because although he only weighed 170 pounds he was a driving runner, a precision passer, and a great blocker. In 1941 he was captain of the Virginia team and maintained his extraordinary record. He was later a member of several pro-football teams as well as playing for Randolph Field, Texas, while he served with the Air Force. He returned to the University as backfield coach in 1947 and again in 1954.

His awards include those of Professional Team All-American, 1942; Service Team All-American, 1944; the Carr Award; and election to the College Football Hall of Fame, 1956, and to the National Football Foundation Hall of Fame at Rutgers.

288.   Ben Martin and Jim Bakhtiar, 1956

Football in the 1950's

Ben Martin, who came to the University in 1956 from his post as chief assistant to the coaching staff at the United States Naval Academy, had an admirable record both scholastically and athletically. He had played football at Princeton and Annapolis, to which he had transferred on appointment, and he also graduated from the Naval Academy as president of his class and with distinction. He left the University to become head coach at the United States Air Force Academy.

Jim Bakhtiar, from Abadan, Iran, was so remarkable at football during his second year at the University that he was named the area's most outstanding football player by the Washington Touchdown Club in 1956. He received a number of other awards during that same year and went on to be the team's captain the next year. After his undergraduate training, he remained at the University to study medicine.

289. The Aviator, by Gutzon
Borglum

The Aviator

One of the best-known statues at the University is that of the *Aviator,* by Gutzon Borglum. It was a gift to the University in 1919 by a group of friends of James Rogers McConnell, who was among the first four pilots of the Lafayette Escadrille to be killed in World War I. McConnell, born in 1887, and an alumnus of the University, volunteered for the French Army in December, 1915. He was decorated with the Croix de Guerre and fell in battle on March 19, 1917. He was a *sergent pilote* and is shown the first on the left in a photograph taken at his base in Luxeuil, the Vosges, France, with three other American volunteers and their captain. The statue bears the inscription "Soaring Like an Eagle, into New Heavens of Valor and Devotion."

290. James McConnell and friends, Luxeuil, Vosges, France

291. New dormitories on Monroe Hill, 1929

Monroe Hill Houses, 1929

In 1928–29 a group of new dormitories was built on Monroe Hill. They were large enough to house 300 students and the individual units within the group were named for former professors at the University—Professors Davis, Gildersleeve, Harrison, Holmes, Long, Mallet, McGuffey, Peters, Rogers, Smith, Tucker, and Venable. The design, with two suites of living room and bedroom sharing a bath, was patterned after that of the housing at the Harvard School of Business by the architects, Walter D. Blair of New York, John K. Peebles of Norfolk, R. E. Lee Taylor of Baltimore, and Edmund S. Campbell of the School of Architecture. The cost of the dormitories was amortized through funds received from room rentals.

Credits

Pictorial History of the University of Virginia

was composed, printed, and bound by Kingsport Press, Inc., Kingsport, Tennessee. The paper is Mohawk Superfine and the types are Bodoni Book and Bodoni 175. Design is by Edward G. Foss.

292.   Aerial view, Copley Hill

Copley Hill

293.   A trailer, Copley Hill

In 1945–46 the University was given a group of surplus house trailers and barracks by the federal government to use as emergency housing for married students, a group which had not been numerous here before World War II. The longevity of these units was startling; although their installation only cost $150,000, they were used for twenty years. Their principal virtue was their nominal rent, for they were uncomfortable, cramped, and in constant danger from fires. Happily these units were at last torn down to make way for University Hall. At Copley Hill there was also a nursery set up by Buildings and Grounds. It may be seen in the foreground of the photograph.

294. Aerial view, McCormick Road Houses

McCormick Road Houses

A series of ten first-year dormitories were built in 1951, the same year as the completion of the new women's dormitory. They were situated on the old golf course (see Illus. 165) and were designed to house 1,244 students by the New York firm of Eggers and Higgins. At the time of construction, it was thought that this vast student housing project, which cost $3,000,000, would serve the University's future adequately, but, of course, many more dormitories have had to be built since. The units were named after the following professors – Bonnycastle, Dabney, Echols, Emmet, Hancock, Humphreys, Kent, Lefevre, Metcalf, and Page.

295. Entrance, McCormick Road Houses

296. Mary Munford Hall

297. The "Glass Hat" and the Alderman Road Houses

Mary Munford Hall

In spite of the designation in 1944 of Mary Washington College in Fredericksburg as the women's division of the University, the number of women students at the University itself made it feasible to complete a dormitory for them in 1951. This half-million-dollar structure was named in honor of Mary Cooke Branch Munford, of Richmond, who had been a long-time adherent of coeducation for women at the University and a member of its Board of Visitors from 1926 to 1938.

The Alderman Road Houses

Hardly a decade after the completion of the McCormick Road Houses, it was found necessary to build yet another dormitory complex. This new group on Alderman Road holds 840 students and was financed by $3,200,000 raised by the sale of revenue bonds to be retired by the rentals received from the dormitories. Dedicated by Professor Robert K. Gooch on May 16, 1964, the individual units in the group are named after Professors Courtenay, Dunglison, Dunnington, Fitzhugh, Lile, Maupin, and Tuttle. Now four more units have been completed (1968), designed by the architects for the original eight, Johnson, Craven, and Gibson. These newest dormitories are named after Professors Balz, Dobie, Webb, and Watson.

298.   Registration day, 1956

Registration Day, 1956

Registration at the University has grown from the simple signing of a name as it was in the beginning to a complicated business that sometimes seems to lead to chaos instead of order. New techniques have recently been introduced, techniques which, in combination with a computer, will perhaps smooth out the difficulties of this tense time for both the student body and the faculty.

299. North entrance of Cabell Hall

300. South entrance of Cabell Hall addition

Cabell Hall

Just as Cabell Hall and the two buildings flanking it became the University's principal classroom complex after the 1895 fire, so has its addition become the classroom center of the post-World War II University. Built in 1951, designed by Eggers and Higgins, and costing over $1,500,000, the addition's lecture halls and offices serve an immense number of students, who are more apt to burst out of it between classes than to enjoy the sun on its steps.

Classrooms

A need for a variety of classrooms has arisen during the twentieth century. Some of these have already been seen. Only a few more can be shown, but the wide range is fully explored in these few from the informality of the history seminar to the concentrated formality of the Graduate School of Business Administration to the rather terrifying amount of technological equipment displayed in the examination at the School of Medicine or the equally formidable amount as seen in the laboratory at the School of Engineering.

301. Graduate history seminar

302. Classroom of the Graduate School of Business Administration

303. Classroom of the School of Medicine

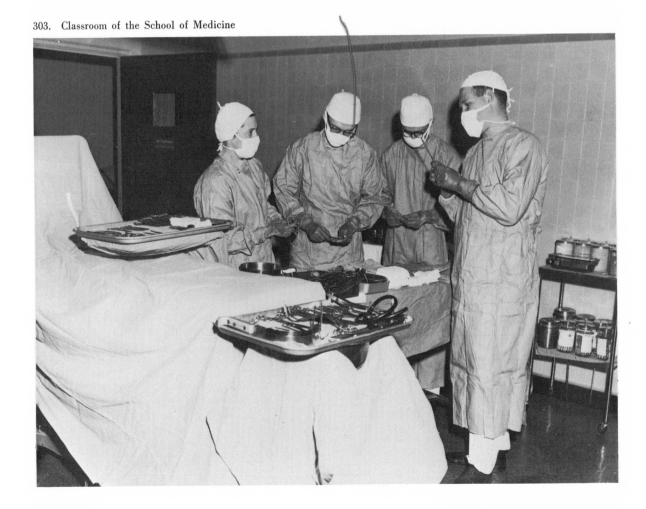

304. Laboratory of the School of Engineering, 1948

305. The Honor Committee, 1964

The Honor Committee

The Honor Committee has been one of the greatest forces for good in the life of the University. The devotion of its members in the execution of their duties and the respect they command in that execution as well as the unquestioning obedience of the students to their decisions have raised the operation of student affairs to a very high level indeed. The honor system, which is entirely administered by students, has been one of the unique features of the University and certainly one of the features of which it is most proud. Although the pledge of honor has been in existence since 1842, the Honor Committee, as such, was not formed until the turn of the twentieth century.

Naval ROTC

After World War II, military
training units remained at the
University, and Tuesday afternoon is drill day. Here the Naval
Reserve Officers Training Corps is
shown in formation in McIntire
Amphitheater. Although this is a
1953 photograph, similar forma-
tions have taken place ever since
as the weekly excursion into military life has become a part of the
student pattern.

306. Naval ROTC, 1953

307. The Corner, 1946

The Corner, 1946

From the days of the bookstore in Temperance Hall (see Illus. 84), the Corner has been the principal shopping center for the student. In this 1946 photograph the present bustle and lack of parking space is anticipated, while the two major focal points, the Anderson Brothers building at the extreme right and the University Cafeteria (with no University sponsorship) at the left, define this commercial adjunct to the University.

Student Organizations

The listing of student organizations in this section has been limited to those established since 1918 that are Greek letter, honorary, or professional. This, of course, omits many that are seriously devoted to fields of study, such as the Classics Club, and some which have been dedicated to play, such as the various Marching Societies. The number of societies is so great that some limitation was necessary. One can only apologize to those groups which have had to be omitted.

SOCIAL FRATERNITIES

Delta Sigma Phi, 1921. Inactive 1933. Reactivated 1965
Delta Upsilon, 1922
Alpha Epsilon Pi, 1924
Tau Kappa Epsilon, 1949
Sigma Phi, 1953
Sigma Pi, 1959
Pi Kappa Phi, 1961

SOCIAL SORORITIES

Chi Omega, 1927. Inactive
Kappa Delta, 1932. Inactive
Zeta Tau Alpha, 1952

HONOR SOCIETY FOR WOMEN

Lychnos Society, 1928

PROFESSIONAL FRATERNITIES

Delta Theta Pi, 1919. Law
Alpha Chi Sigma, 1922. Chemistry and chemical engineering
Alpha Rho Chi, 1922. Architecture
Phi Chi, 1922. Medicine
Theta Tau, 1923. Engineering
Trigon, 1924. Engineering
Delta Sigma Pi, 1925. Business
Scarab, 1928. Architecture
Pi Delta Epsilon, 1940. Journalism
Phi Delta Kappa, (?). Education.

HONORARY ORGANIZATIONS

Alpha Omega Alpha, 1919. Medical honor society
Tau Beta Pi, 1921. National honorary engineering fraternity
Sigma Xi, 1924. National honorary society for science, pure and applied
Omicron Delta Kappa, 1925. National honor society
Alpha Phi Omega, 1929. Reactivated, 1962. National service fraternity
Beta Gamma Sigma, 1929. Honorary society for commerce and business administration
Sigma Gamma Epsilon, 1952. National honorary earth science society
Eta Kappa Nu, 1957. National honorary society for electrical engineers
Phi Sigma Society, 1958. National earth science honorary society
Alpha Epsilon Delta, 1964. International premedical honor society
Sigma Pi Sigma, 1966. Honor society for undergraduate students in physics
Delta Sigma Rho-Tau Kappa Alpha. National honorary society of debators
Sigma Delta Pi. National honor society for those studying Spanish and Spanish culture

Epilogue

308.   The future of the University

The Future of the University

Not only has the University continued to expand under President Shannon, but his plans for the future envision continued growth, both intellectually and physically. Here he is shown explaining some of that desired future growth with the aid of a large aerial photograph of the University.

Credits

E. M. Betts Collection, Manuscripts Division, University of Virginia Library:

5, 52, 61, 62, 65, 70, 71, 72, 74, 77, 78, 79, 80, 81, 82, 84, 123, 125, 126, 131, 133 (from Richmond *Dispatch*, Oct. 28, 1895), 134, 137, 138, 157, 162 (from Anderson Bros., *University of Virginia: Photogravures*), 163, 164 (gift of Miss Anna Barringer), 165, 166 (gift of Miss Anna Barringer), 169

Mrs. E. M. Betts:

88, 101, 108, 112, 117, 118, 122, 132, 135, 168 (gift of Miss Anne Capler), 171, 208, 213, 214, 229

Samuel Chamberlain:

113, 161, 193, 200, 206

Corks and Curls:

1890, 175; *1892*, 92, 93, 94, 95, 96, 97, 98, 99; *1893*, 128; *1894*, 120; *1895*, 172, 176; *1899*, 177; *1901*, 178; *1902*, 141, 184, 185, 186, 187, 188, 189; *1905*, 179, 180, 181, 182; *1911*, 183

Department of Graphics, University of Virginia:

48 (original portrait in Cabell Hall), 50 (original portrait in Colonnade Club), 58 (original portrait in Clark Memorial Hall), 75, 114, 238, 239, 291

Information Services, University of Virginia:

2, 68, 69, 86, 107, 111, 143, 146, 190, 192, 194, 207, 209, 210, 211, 212, 215, 216, 217, 218, 219, 220, 221, 225, 227, 230, 232, 233, 234, 235, 236, 237, 239, 240, 242, 243, 244, 245, 246, 247, 248, 249, 251, 252, 253, 254, 255, 257, 264, 265, 275, 276, 278, 281, 282, 283, 284, 285, 289, 292, 293, 294, 295, 296, 297, 299, 300, 301, 302, 303, 305

Manuscripts Division, University of Virginia Library:

1, 8, 9, 10 (from microfilm of original in Thomas Jefferson Papers, Library of Congress), 11, 12, 13, 14, 15, 16, 17, 18, 19 (from *The White House Gallery of Official Portraits of the Presidents*, comp. G. R. Devitt [Washington, D.C., 1907]), 20, 22, 23, 24, 25, 26, 27, 28, 29, 30, 31, 32, 33, 34, 35, 36, 37, 38, 39, 40, 41, 42, 43, 45, 46, 49 (original portrait in Pavilion VIII), 51 (from *National Portrait Gallery of Distinguished Americans* [Philadelphia, 1854], III), 53 (original portrait in Gilmer Hall), 54 (original portrait in University of Virginia Library), 55 (original portrait in School of Medicine), 56 (original engraving of the lost portrait in Thomas Addis Emmet, *The Emmet Family* [New York, 1898]), 57, 59, 60, 63 (from *Harper's New Monthly Magazine*, Aug. 1856), 64 (from Faculty Minutes, Oct. 1, 1842, VI, 34), 66, 67, 76, 83, 89, 90, 91, 100, 102, 103, 104, 106, 109, 110, 115, 116, 119, 121, 124, 127, 129 (from *University of Virginia: Photogravures* [Charlottesville: Anderson Bros., 1895]), 136, 139, 140 (from *Alumni Bulletin*, Feb. 1896), 142 (from *Alumni Bulletin*, Feb. 1896), 144, 145, 147, 148, 149, 150, 151, 156 (original portrait in Jefferson Hall), 158 (original portrait in University of Virginia Library), 159, 160 (original photograph in Jefferson Hall), 167, 170, 173, 174, 191, 199, 223, 241, 256, 258, 259, 261, 262, 263, 266, 267, 268, 270, 271, 272, 273, 277, 279, 280, 286, 287, 288, 290, 298, 306, 308

The Thomas Jefferson Memorial Foundation:

7, 21, 260

University of Virginia Alumni Association:

105, 130, 153, 154, 155, 195, 196, 197, 198, 201, 202, 203, 204, 205, 222, 226, 228, 231, 269, 274, 304, 307

Others:

4 from the Collections of the Maryland Historical Society; 6 courtesy of Mr. Donald B. Straus of New York City; 44 courtesy of the Art Commission of The City of New York; 47 courtesy of the New York State Historical Association; 73 from H. M. Pierce Gallagher, *Robert Mills, Architect of the Washington Monument, 1781–1855* (New York: Columbia University Press, 1935); 85 from Paul Brandon Barringer *et al.*, *University of Virginia* (New York, 1904), I; 87 from *McGuffey's Eclectic Spelling-Book* (rev. ed.; Cincinnati and New York, 1879); 152 from *University of Virginia: Views of the Grounds and Buildings* (supplement to *University of Virginia Record*, XX [1934]); 224 from Judge Advocate General's School; 250 by Ed Roseberry

Pictorial History of the University of Virginia

was composed, printed, and bound by Kingsport Press, Inc., Kingsport, Tennessee. The paper is Mohawk Superfine and the types are Bodoni Book and Bodoni 175. Design is by Edward G. Foss.